MORE PRAISE FOR *THE S*

"*The Secrets of Power Selling* packs high [...] readable format. Read it and reap Kelley Robertson's considerable experience and wisdom."
Jim Clemmer, President, The Clemmer Group

"I have had the pleasure of reading every article that you have published as well as frequenting your web site for interesting business tips. After working with you directly and witnessing the success that you were able to evoke from our retail franchisee chain, it was with excitement and pleasure that I read through *The Secrets of Power Selling*. The format of this book made every chapter exciting and easy to use. As you move through the various Power Selling Tips you can feel yourself growing in strength and confidence. The chapters are also set up in a manner that will enable the reader to use them as a training tool. I look forward to incorporating them into our company's training guidelines."
Catherine Deslippe, Vice President Operations, Nutrition House

"Having a small business, I have to be everything, including the salesperson. Unfortunately, I don't have the time to go to a seminar on every area in which I need to become proficient. Having spent my career as a technical person who had avoided being involved in the sales process, I am a beginner with regard to doing sales, so this is an especially weak area of mine. This is why I found Kelley Robertson's book *The Secrets of Power Selling* to be a perfect fit for my purposes. Each topic is short so that I never have an excuse that I can't make time to read one. They're organized in a way that I can jump to those I think I particularly need help with or return to one, again. In addition, Kelley's examples are practical and lead me through the actions I need to take. Through *The Secrets of Power Selling* Kelley is opening up an understanding of the world of sales—a world I previously thought to be mysterious."
Gloria Metrick, GeoMetrick Enterprises

"*The Secrets of Power Selling* has practical day-to-day applications for anyone who deals with customers and sales. The layout makes it easy to reference and a valuable resource that all sales professionals will benefit from. A must read."
Tyler Bradford, President, Advanced Expeditions

"As a seasoned sales professional, I really enjoyed *The Secrets of Power Selling*. I found more than a few strategies and tips that can immediately create more return on investment for my sales efforts. The chapters are clear, concise and perfectly self-contained so you can reference and read at will without worrying about missing important information. Each chapter is a topic unto itself and includes many practical suggestions and tips that are 'ready to use' and applicable to most sales positions and organizations. I would recommend *The Secrets of Power Selling* as a must-read for any sales professional truly serious about maximizing their potential."

Bill Nutter, Managing Partner, The Delta Synergy Group

"I've been in sales for over 22 years and have read many books on sales. *The Secrets of Power Selling* captures the essence of sales and all its key factors in an easy-to-read, straightforward style. This book is an excellent resource for anyone in sales. It's a great refresher for those experienced in the sales profession and reinforces the important aspects of the sales process that sometimes get overlooked. It is the perfect resource for any small to medium size business as not only the true salesperson can benefit from Kelley's wonderful insight, but also all the non-traditional sales-related personnel who may have contact with any customers."

Steve Whigham, Co-CEO, Promotional Elements Inc.

"I recommend this book to any sales professional who wants to reach a higher level of success. Every chapter offers practical, common-sense ways to hone your skills and achieve improved results immediately. When preparing for important sales meetings, I use this book as a refresher to make sure I'm ready to handle any direction the conversation might take. It has dramatically increased my confidence and my sales success! You owe it to yourself to read this book now. It is packed full of ideas to improve your results, regardless of your sales experience."

Patricia Hobbs, President, Direct Path Inc.

"Kelley has been there and done it and that's why this book is a must read. As a master facilitator and trainer, Kelley gets right down to the nitty gritty of creating customer comfort and prospecting not only with your brain, but also with your heart. Learn to apply what Kelley tells you in *The Secrets of Power Selling* and you'll find your roadmap to selling success."

Brian Larter, President, Larter Advertising

THE SECRETS OF
POWER
SELLING

THE SECRETS OF POWER SELLING

101 TIPS
TO HELP YOU IMPROVE YOUR SALES RESULTS

KELLEY ROBERTSON

John Wiley & Sons Canada, Ltd.

National Library of Canada Cataloguing in Publication Data

Robertson, Kelley
    The secrets of power selling : 101 tips to help you improve your sales results / Kelley Robertson.

ISBN 978-0-470-83942-3

    1. Selling. I. Title.

HF5438.25.R6194 2007   658.85   C2006-904104-0

Production Credits:
Cover and interior text design: Jason Vandenberg
Wiley Bicentennial Logo: Richard J. Pacifico
Printer: Friesens

John Wiley & Sons Canada, Ltd.
6045 Freemont Blvd.
Mississauga, Ontario
L5R 4J3

Printed in Canada

1 2 3 4 5 FP 11 10 09 08 07

CONTENTS

INTRODUCTION

The majority of sales books on the market focus on a specific topic or aspect of selling. Others provide a complete overview of the sales process. You can read books on prospecting, cold calling, generating referrals, selling to executives, and closing techniques, as well as dozens—if not hundreds—of different ways to sell.

This book is a bit different.

If you are like most sales professionals, you are very busy. You probably do not have time to read an entire book in one sitting. That's why I have deliberately kept the chapters in this book brief and focused. Each chapter concentrates on providing information on a specific aspect and single topic of achieving sales success. From asking questions, to planning, to establishing trust, each of the chapters offers practical advice that can be used to improve your sales.

This format allows you to read the chapters that most appeal to you and that will have the best impact on your results.

Enjoy!

THE POWER OF
ADAPTING YOUR APPROACH

"The ability to connect with people is a key sales trait."
Kelley Robertson

Every person you interact with is different. That means you need to adapt your approach if you want to maximize your results. You cannot deal with a multitude of people, using the same style all the time, and hope to achieve the best results. Adapting your approach means you need to be aware of different personality styles.

In 1928, Dr. William Moulton Marston created the foundation for what is now known as the DiSC profile, one of the best known and most widely used behavioral styles assessment tools. The DiSC profile represents four distinct styles—dominant (driver), influencer (expressive), steadiness (amiable), and compliant (analytical). Here is a summary of each style, how to recognize each, and the most effective way to approach each style.

The Dominant or Driver: A problem- and goal-oriented person who is focused on achieving results. These individuals tend to be forceful, bottom-line people who hate to waste time. They want straight talk and direct answers. You can recognize Drivers by their directness and sometimes bluntness, their tendency to use "I" in their conversation, and their body language. Drivers will often sit forward, point with their forefinger as they speak to take control or emphasize. They will interrupt the conversation while maintaining very direct eye contact. They will have a strong handshake, and their workspace will likely be disorganized. Their voice-mail message will be curt and brief: *"This is Joanne. Leave a message and I'll call you back."*

SALES TIP

Focus on showing them how they will get results and achieve their goals. Use the word "you" several times in your conversation. Allow them to dominate the sales discussion, ask for their opinion, and let them express their ideas and thoughts. This will help you gain their buy-in. Limit the amount of small talk during your meeting because these individuals want to get down to business quickly. Maintain a high level of confidence and do not be intimidated by their directness.

The Influencer or Expressive: A people-focused, fast-paced person with lots of energy. Their key strength is to promote ideas and persuade others to agree with them. They have a tendency to "tell" people versus "asking." Expressive individuals are very concerned with rejection. Their workspace will often be covered with pictures, awards, or letters. They usually demonstrate a friendly but firm handshake. These individuals are the easiest to spot because they are optimistic and friendly. Their voice-mail message will likely be long and friendly: *"This is Robert. I'm out meeting clients right now so I can't take your call. Please leave me a message and I'll call you back. Thanks for calling and have a great day!"*

SALES TIP

Image is very important to Expressives so praise them and show how your product will make them look good in front of their peers, co-workers, business partners, and customers. Use third-party testimonials and endorsements and tell stories during your sales presentation.

The Steadiness or Amiable: An Amiable is most concerned about helping other people and works at a steady pace. They will be much more quiet and reserved than a Driver or an Expressive, which makes them more difficult to read. They may not say anything if they disagree with you so as not to create conflict. They are excellent listeners and prefer discussions with one or two people versus group conversations. Their workspace is typically well-organized and clean. They are also hesitant to make changes because they enjoy consistency and routine. Their voice-mail message will be soft and possibly apologetic: *"Hi, this is Cheryl. I'm very sorry I missed your call. Please leave me a message and I will make sure I call you back."*

SALES TIP

Demonstrate how easy the change will be to incorporate into their work environment and how it will help the other people on the team. Use the word "team" in your presentation. Soften your tone of voice and slow down your rate of speech.

The Compliant or Analytical: These people are critical thinkers and draw conclusions based on facts, figures, accuracy, and the rules. They focus on procedures. Perfection is very important to them. They are not necessarily shy but they can be difficult to read because they do not show their feelings. Their workspace will be very precise and neat; in some cases, everything will be organized alphabetically and labeled. Analytical individuals prefer information in writing, so send them an agenda prior to a meeting. Use bullet points in your correspondence, and make sure your spelling and punctuation are 100 percent accurate. Their voice-mail message will ask you to leave a detailed message: *"This is Geoff. Please leave your name, phone number, time of your call, the reason for your call, and the best time to contact you."*

SALES TIP

Give this person time to make a decision and back up your information with lots of facts, figures, and statistics. Be precise and avoid using generalities or discussing feelings. Above all, avoid trying to push this person into making a quick decision. Highlight referrals and satisfied customers to help reduce the risk factor.

When you adapt your natural style to more closely match the style of your customer you will gain rapport more quickly. This means you will experience less resistance and you will increase the likelihood of moving the sales process forward, providing of course, that your product or service is of value to your customer's company or organization.

THE POWER OF AFFIRMATIONS

"It's the repetition of affirmations that leads to belief. And once that belief becomes a deep conviction, things begin to happen."
Claude M. Bristol, *The Magic of Believing*

Being confident is key to success in sales, but it's not always easy to feel this way. Developing the skill of using positive self-talk or affirmations can boost not only your self-image, but also your success in your job. An affirmation is a powerful tool that will help you develop personal self-confidence, reprogram your thinking, and achieve better results. Simply put, affirmations are positive statements that we repeat to ourselves frequently.

Although many people are familiar with this concept, few actually use it on a regular basis. You may remember the *Saturday Night Live* skit that satirized affirmations. The character would look at himself in a mirror while stating a variety of affirmations, concluding with, "Gosh darn, I like myself." The truth is that affirmations really do work. They are designed to replace feelings of inferiority, doubt, and the lack of self-worth. The way they work is simple; there are only three rules that you need to remember.

1. **Affirmations must be personal.** When you develop an affirmation begin with "I." For example, "I am a successful salesperson."

2. **State affirmations in the present tense.** Avoid saying, "I want to quit smoking." This states your desire, not your intended result. Instead, state, "I enjoy the lifestyle of a non-smoker."

3. **Affirmations must be positive.** Avoid using negative words. For instance, "I don't want to gain more weight" should be phrased as, "I look great in my new suit."

The next important point of affirmations is that you must repeat them aloud several times a day. You must drive this message deep into your subconscious and replace the other thoughts that occupy your brain with it. The most effective way to do this is through repetition. The more often you repeat an affirmation the more your subconscious goes to work to produce it and make it become a reality.

Here is an example. When I was in my thirties, I decided to quit smoking. I created several affirmations that reflected the outcome I imagined. "I am a nonsmoker." "I enjoy a smoke-free life." "I live the lifestyle of a nonsmoker." "I enjoy living as a nonsmoker." I repeated these affirmations several times a day, long before the deadline I had set. A few months later I did quit, almost five months sooner than I had originally intended. I also continued to repeat these affirmations for the first month or two afterward to help me get through the withdrawal period. Affirmations helped me picture myself as a nonsmoker. They helped my subconscious mind make it a reality. For someone who smoked for more than twenty years, this was a challenging picture to create.

You can use affirmations to develop self-confidence in selling. Create a variety of affirmations such as

- "I am a successful salesperson"
- "I am confident and comfortable on sales calls"
- "I enjoy selling"
- "I like helping people make buying decisions"
- "Selling is a rewarding career"
- "Selling is an honorable profession."

Repeat these statements aloud to yourself several times a day and you will soon notice a change in your behavior.

SALES TIP

If you are currently earning $25,000 a year and your goal is to earn $100,000, you must break this goal into digestible, bite-size chunks first. Don't make that $75,000 leap in one affirmation; your conscious mind will not accept it as being possible. Instead, create several affirmations. Start with the goal of increasing your income to $35,000. Once you achieve this, create a new affirmation with your income at $50,000, and then $75,000. Then make the jump to the final figure. You'll find taking the smaller steps much more effective than trying to make a huge jump all at once. However, once you begin to build momentum, you can take larger steps to achieve your goal. Be patient. Before long, you will notice the change gradually beginning to happen.

THE POWER OF APOLOGIES

*"An apology is the superglue of life.
It can repair just about anything."*
Lynn Johnston

We all make mistakes. As simple as this seems, most people do not admit to the mistakes they make. Instead, they try to cover them up or redirect the blame. However, the best salespeople admit their mistakes.

An interesting phenomenon has occurred in the business world in the last few years. More corporate executives fail to admit fault even when they and/or their company have clearly been in the wrong. Yet, people will accept mistakes providing they feel that the people who have committed the wrongdoing are sorry for their actions. A classic example of this is Bill Clinton's affair with intern Monica Lewinsky. The general public accepted that even the President of the United States was susceptible to making a mistake, providing he confessed to it.

Issuing an apology is a challenging process for most people. Many sales professionals feel that they will lose client confidence if they admit to making a mistake. Yet these same individuals will impress the importance of telling the truth on their children.

As a business owner, I have had to apologize to customers from time to time (no, my business does not run flawlessly!) and I have no hesitation in doing so. I have yet to have people tell me they will no longer do business with me because I have admitted to making a mistake.

However, I can think of several companies I will not give my business to because they failed to apologize for a mistake they made.

An extremely powerful approach is to apologize before your customer knows something is wrong. Let's say, for example, you promised delivery of a product to a customer by a specific date. You later learn that the shipping of the item has been delayed. Instead of waiting for your customer to contact you after the original delivery date has passed, take a proactive approach and call your customer to advise her of the change. Although you did not cause the problem, you should accept responsibility for it—after all, you *are* the company, in your customer's eyes. Many salespeople are concerned about this strategy because they fear losing the sale. While this will happen from time to time, in most cases your customers will appreciate your proactive approach. Plus, they will respect the fact that you accepted responsibility for the situation.

Keep your apology brief. Tell your customer that you are sorry for the mistake, and state what corrective action you plan to take. Then follow through and make sure you do what you say you will. A common mistake many people make is to apologize too much. This means explaining exactly what went wrong, what caused the problem, or why the situation happened. People don't really care about this—all they want is a solution. Here is an example:

"Mrs. Smith, I'm very sorry for the delay in getting back to you and resolving your service issue. I have made arrangements for a service person to contact you today to arrange a suitable time to visit your site and correct the problem. He should be contacting you within the hour. If, for whatever reason he doesn't call you, please call me immediately. My direct line is..."

SALES TIP

The next time something happens by mistake with one of your clients, take the time to apologize, solve the problem, and follow up to make sure it was resolved properly.

THE POWER OF APPEARANCE

"We tend to evaluate others on the basis of physical, outward appearance."
Marvin J. Ashton

Whether we like it or not, our appearance will affect our sales results. That does not mean you have to dress in a two-thousand-dollar suit, but it is critical that you look professional regardless of what you sell. My personal belief is that you should dress one step higher than your client. It is easier to tone down your appearance during a meeting by removing your jacket or tie than it is to step it up.

I once attended a conference for networking purposes—many decision-makers for my target market were in attendance. The stated dress code was business casual but I decided I would wear a shirt and tie. Imagine my surprise when I arrived and noticed that most of the attendees were attired in suits. Even though I was overdressed according to the stated dress code, I actually ended up being underdressed!

Here are a few guidelines to bear in mind with respect to your appearance.

- Avoid garish jewelry unless that is the kind of business you are in.

- Limit your use of colognes and fragrances. Many people are easily offended by perfumes and some are even allergic to them. If you do wear a fragrance, keep it light; don't overdo it.

- Keep your nails and hair neatly trimmed and clean.

- Never chew gum!

- If you smoke, wash your face and hands immediately after you have a cigarette. The smoke lingers on clothing and skin, and many people find it offensive. Never smoke immediately before a sales call with a new client or prospect.

- Brush your teeth throughout the day. This will help keep your breath fresh, especially if you drink coffee or smoke.

- Dry-clean your shirts or blouses rather than machine-wash them. They will look brighter, fresher, and crisper. Even the hottest iron can't compete with pressure steam. Have your suits and ties dry-cleaned regularly too. Suits should only be dry-cleaned three to four times a year, so hang them outside for a few hours each month to keep them fresh.

- Make sure that your clothing fits you well. Properly hemmed pants or skirts, jackets with the correct sleeve length, and shirts with the right collar size, or blouses that fit properly all contribute to your professional appearance.

- Invest in good shoes and keep them polished. Many people gauge a salesperson by the quality of his or her shoes. Buff them daily to maintain a lasting shine and replace shoes that are worn out or severely scuffed.

- Avoid clothing that is worn out. We all have a favorite shirt, sweater, dress, or jacket. Nevertheless, there comes a point at which even our favorite article of clothing becomes too worn or outdated for business use. Recognize when your clothing needs to be replaced and do it.

Although these may seem like commonsense suggestions, many salespeople often neglect or overlook them. A general rule of thumb to follow: the more expensive the products you sell, the more professional your appearance should be.

SALES TIP

Post the tips listed on these two pages and review them as you prepare for your next sales call.

THE POWER OF ARTICLES

"My aim is to put down on paper what I see and what I feel in the best and simplest way."
Ernest Hemingway

Writing articles is one of the most effective ways to establish yourself as an expert. Articles give you great exposure both in print and online, and writing an article is easier than you think.

Most trade publications are hungry for content. When my first book was released, I was contacted by a trade magazine to write a regular column for them. Since then, I have expanded my writing and now submit articles to several hundred publications—paper and web-based. I have booked many workshops and speaking engagements as a direct result of someone reading one of these articles.

You may feel that this strategy does not apply to your industry. I know many people who write, including real estate agents, people who sell vending services, financial planners, marketing experts, professional speakers, virtual assistants, publicists, retailers, health-supplement manufacturers, just to name a few. Regardless of what you sell and to whom, articles can help get you noticed by prospective customers. Writing articles can help you establish yourself as an expert. However, any article you write must address the concerns of your target market. This means that you need to consider what problems your target audience faces and write an article that offers suggestions to deal with these issues. You may also feel that you can't write a lengthy article that people will read. Here are some tips that will help you get started:

- Start with a main point or topic. Let's say you sell industrial farm equipment. You could easily write articles about proper maintenance of the equipment, as well as some tips and techniques to maximize the use and life span of specific products. Your article could be, *Eight Ways to Extend the Life of Your Tractor*.

- Think of six or eight key points that are relevant to your topic. The average article in a trade magazine is six hundred to one thousand words, so write a hundred words (about two paragraphs) for each key point. Using the tractor example, you would elaborate on each of the eight ways to extend the life of a tractor. In some cases, you will find that you can write an entire article about one single point.

- Create an opening or introduction, and close with a call to action. Write in a conversational tone rather than a formal one. It can help if you picture the typical person who will be reading the article and imagine that you are writing to that person.

- Write a byline or author bio that states who you are, what you do and for whom, and how to contact you—telephone and e-mail. To drive more traffic to your web site I also recommend that you offer something to the reader. For example, my byline states that people can receive a free copy of *100 Ways to Increase Your Sales* by sub-scribing to my newsletter, available at my web-site.

You're done! You will find that it is easier to write at certain times than others. Sometimes I have written an entire article in less than thirty minutes while in other situations it has taken me the better part of a day to get the words on paper. Regardless, this is still a very powerful way to market and promote yourself and your business.

One final word: make sure that the articles you write offer something of value to the reader. They should not be a blatant advertisement for you and your company.

SALES TIP

1. Make a list of topics about which you could write an article. Sketch out a few key points for an article, then expand on each one.

2. Invest thirty minutes researching magazines that your target market might read and send a quick e-mail to the editor outlining your article idea. The key benefits of writing articles include
   - establishing yourself as an expert in the marketplace,
   - generating new business leads,
   - creating awareness of your business,
   - driving more traffic to your web site, and
   - creating a pull system of marketing.

THE POWER OF ASKING FOR HELP

"If you don't swallow your pride and you try to tough it out in an area where you lack skill, knowledge or experience, you exponentially increase the likelihood you will fail."
Dave Lorenzo, *Career Intensity*

No one can achieve true success or full potential on his or her own. We all need other people to help us along the way. However, the majority of salespeople do not ask for assistance, and try to do everything themselves.

Prior to starting my business, I contacted many other people who operated similar businesses. I wanted to know what challenges they encountered, what mistakes they made, and what advice they would give someone who was beginning a business. Everyone I contacted was helpful and willing to share his or her experiences. I took notes and referred to them as I planned my strategy. I also read dozens of books that were related to my business. Last, I approached a well-respected businessperson, discussed my plans with him, and asked his advice. I listened carefully to what he told me and worked at implementing his ideas.

Several years later, I constantly talk to other sales professionals, small business owners, sales trainers, and authors. I have learned that I don't know everything. (Ouch! That was hard to admit!) However, I do know that I want to be successful in my business, and talking to other people gives me additional insights.

Several friends of mine have operated their own training companies for many years, and I would be foolish not to listen to their experiences and learn from their mistakes. Their philosophies and the way in which they run their businesses may be different than mine, but they have wisdom and expertise that will help me in my business.

Asking for help is not a sign of weakness. In fact, it is a show of strength. It takes courage to ask for help.

It can be challenging for many people to ask for help, especially from peers. Here is a method of starting the conversation.

"Hi June. I'm meeting a new prospect next week and they are much larger than my typical client. I know that you have a lot of experience dealing with large organizations and wondered if you could help me understand some of the challenges that big companies face so that I can better position my solution."

I have encountered very few people who are unwilling to respond to this request. The reason is simple: most successful people want others to be successful as well. If you are not comfortable asking someone in your personal network, consider joining a chat room or online forum. A quick Internet search will usually help you find a forum or group of people who share similar challenges. Many members of these forums are experts and are willing to share their expertise with you. One word of caution, however. Be prepared to give advice and feedback in addition to seeking it. I have participated in some online groups and some people repeatedly ask for help without reciprocating.

SALES TIP

The next time you encounter a challenge or obstacle in your business that you are not sure how to handle, contact someone in your network who may have experienced a similar situation. Describe your problem and ask if they can offer any suggestions that will help you.

THE POWER OF ASKING FOR THE SALE

"You ask, you get. You don't ask, you don't get.
If you don't learn to ask for the sale, you're going to go broke."
Hank Trisler, *No Bull Selling*

I have learned from experience that many people expect you to ask them to make a buying decision. Surprisingly, the majority of salespeople fail to ask for the sale. Instead, they wait for their prospect to say something like, "I'll take it," or, "Let's go ahead with this." However, failing to ask a customer for a commitment usually results in lost sales opportunities.

This hesitation is usually caused by our concern about appearing pushy or our fear of rejection. It is natural to want other people to like us. It is a basic human need. However, I have yet to encounter someone getting upset just because he or she was asked to make a buying commitment in a professional manner.

Recognize that buyers expect you to ask for the sale. They know that it's your job to ask for their business. And, in many situations, they *want* you to ask. A few years ago a participant in one of my workshops told me of a sales encounter with a businessman to whom he was selling a television. This sales associate invested the time qualifying the prospect and showed a TV that met the customer's desired needs. Approximately thirty minutes elapsed, and the customer was standing silently in front of the television with his hands thrust deeply in his pockets. A barrage of questions and concerns raced through the sales associate's mind as he tried to figure out what to do next. Finally, he blurted out, "Is there anything else I can do?" The customer looked at him intently for a few moments then replied, "You can ask me if I want it." After the sales associate picked himself up off the floor, he asked for, and closed, the sale.

Another method of dealing with your personal hesitations is to ensure that you've followed the sales process. Gather as much information as you can, and learn exactly what the customer needs and wants. Adapt your sales dialogue to meet the specific issues of each customer. Give her a reason to buy from you. If you have done everything you should have, you will be confident in asking for the sale. Remember that people want to buy from confident salespeople.

Here are several comfortable ways to ask for the sale:

- "How would you like to proceed?"
- "What would you like to do now?"
- "Can I wrap that up for you?"
- "Which option do you prefer?"
- "When do you want this delivered?"
- "Is this acceptable?"
- "When would be a convenient time to schedule this?"
- "What payment plan works best for you?"
- "What is the best way to proceed from here?"
- "Would you like me to start the paperwork?"
- "Are you comfortable with proceeding?"
- "What are the next steps?"

At first, it seems very aggressive to ask the other person to make a buying decision. I still recall my first sales call even though it was many years ago. I met with the manager of a business and presented my services. During our meeting she expressed a high level of interest. I wasn't sure how to proceed (I did not have any formal sales training at that point) so I summoned up the courage and asked, "Would you like to schedule a day for that?" To my surprise, she readily agreed.

The key is to develop a variety of statements and questions that gain this commitment. You will notice an immediate increase in your sales as soon as you start asking for the business.

SALES TIP

Create a list of questions you can ask that will help you move the sale forward. Recite these questions aloud until they feel comfortable rolling off your tongue. Then, use one of them during your next sales call or meeting.

THE POWER OF BARTERING

*"Barter: the direct exchange of goods or services—
without an intervening medium of exchange or money"*
Encyclopaedia Britannica

Negotiating is a common practice in today's business world. Far too often, people focus strictly on the dollars and cents of the process instead of looking at alternate solutions. One such solution is bartering.

I have learned that many organizations—large and small—are willing to trade goods and services in exchange for something they want or need. While you can't use this approach in every sales situation, there is an abundance of times when you can. Here are some examples.

A friend of mine worked with a shopping center and was told that her proposal exceeded their budget by several hundred dollars. My friend asked for that figure in mall gift certificates, and they accepted.

I know people who have exchanged articles for advertisements in magazines; the articles help give them additional exposure in their marketplace. Another friend of mine belongs to a barter exchange group. Members collect barter dollars by exchanging their goods and services, and my friend has enjoyed limousine rides as well as photography and a variety of other services.

I was negotiating a deal with a video-rental company, and they asked me for a fifteen-percent discount on my fee. Instead of immediately granting it, I asked for the comparable amount in movie rentals.

Even large corporations are willing to barter. A business owner I know gave his services to a large company in exchange for one of their high-end products. The company agreed to this because the value of the product was comparable to the services received, but their actual cost of the product was considerably less. So, in the end the company ended up saving money and my friend received a product that he wanted.

SALES TIP

The next time someone balks at the price of your product or service, consider their product offering, and if they have something that appeals to you, ask them if they would consider an exchange.

THE POWER OF BEING YOURSELF

"We all have individual strengths that can help us succeed."
Kelley Robertson

While it is important to learn from others and constantly modify your approach, it is also critical that you be yourself when talking to customers and prospects. I often notice that salespeople change their tone of voice when speaking with customers. In an office supply store I frequent, I often hear a particular sales associate interact with customers. When she speaks to customers, her voice goes up several octaves, and it sounds unnatural.

I see many salespeople mimic or copy someone else in order to close more sales. While I believe that you should tap into the strengths of other people, I believe that you should adapt these techniques to fit your own style. When you try to incorporate another person's style with your own, the result is often less than satisfactory, usually because that particular approach may not feel comfortable to you. You need to modify it, to make it your own.

It is important to allow your natural personality to shine through in your discussions with customers. You are unique individuals, and as such, have your own character to bring to the sales interaction. When you focus on being yourself, you come across as more relaxed and comfortable in the sales process. In turn, your customer will feel more comfortable and more inclined to buy from you. If you have a natural sense of humor, let it flow—providing the humor is appropriate.

SALES TIP

Focus on relaxing during your next sales interaction. Too many salespeople focus on closing the sale, which increases their stress level and prevents them from moving the sale forward. However, when you relax and concentrate on learning more about the customer's situation, you change your focus from "me" to "you."

THE POWER OF BELIEF

> *"Whether you think you can or you think you can't,*
> *you are absolutely right."*
> Henry Ford

Your success stems from your personal belief in your ability to achieve it. Self-limiting beliefs are the single biggest killer of sales careers. I recall one workshop I conducted; several of the participants worked in a retail store. They lamented the fact that they "knew" they wouldn't close any sales in the first hour of business because they "knew" all the people who came into their store were just gathering information so they could buy the product at the competitor down the road. Another participant spoke up and said that this belief system would definitely prevent them from achieving their goals.

Virtually every successful person in business, sports, or entertainment has an unwavering belief in his or her ability to succeed. Not succeeding is not an option they consider, and even when they experience setbacks or failures, they view these situations differently than most people. They think big! They don't settle for average or mediocre. They set lofty goals and expect to achieve them.

Earl Nightingale said, "You become what you think about." When you continually concentrate on the results you want to achieve instead of the roadblocks, obstacles, and barriers, you break through personal limitations. The more positive and confident you are about achieving your goals, the faster you will attract the people, events, and opportunities to make your goals happen.

SALES TIP

Decide now that you will no longer allow self-limitations to hold you back from achieving your goals, sales, and dreams.

THE POWER OF BENEFITS

"F-words (fact, features, functions) only appeal to a few prospects."
Anthony Parinello, *Stop Cold Calling Forever!*

Although many salespeople are taught to use the FAB approach (Feature, Advantage, Benefit) when presenting their product and/or service, most of them talk only about the features. The drawback with this approach is that people buy benefits, not features. People want to know what a specific feature will do for them, and talking about features does not meet this goal.

A feature/benefit statement consists of stating the feature followed by an explanation of what that means to the customer. Here is an example: "Mr. Prospect, we provide your team with a toll-free number for you to contact our tech support at any time after the installation of the system (feature). You will always have someone who can answer your team's questions. That means they will become more proficient with the system in less time (benefit)."

The benefit *must* answer the question, "So what?" Remember, the customer wants to know what's in it for her. Don't waste time talking about things that are unimportant to her. Instead, focus your attention on telling her what she will gain from using your product or service. How can she save time or reduce costs, overhead, or turnover? How will her sales or bottom line be affected?

I recall speaking to another professional speaker and when I asked how companies would benefit by having him work with their employees he stated that they would be more motivated. I kept asking, "So what? How will the organization benefit?" Eventually, we determined that the key benefit he offered was that employees who were injured would spend less time on disability leave. That meant that an average company could save thousands of dollars for each employee who experienced a work-related injury.

I recommend that you list the features of each of your products and services. Beside each feature, record the benefit of the particular feature. Use the format below as a guideline.

Feature:_____

Description:_____

Benefit: That means_____

_____

Here is an example of how the process sounds.

"Mr. Prospect, our training programs are highly interactive. We use a variety of processes, including small and large group discussions and real-life activities that simulate the challenges your employees actually face in their work environment. Your team will have the opportunity to share ideas with each other and practise the new skills, which means they will be able to apply the concepts from the workshop when they return to work. This means you will experience a better return on your investment and see noticeable results immediately."

Lastly, beware of the "feature dump." Don't make the mistake of listing every feature when talking to your customer. This approach is not effective and is a sure way to lose your prospect's interest in your presentation. Instead, focus on explaining only the features that are relevant to each customer's specific situation.

SALES TIP

Using the format given in this chapter, list the key benefits of your products and services, making sure they address the "So what?" question. When you are finished, practise reciting the full statement (feature, description, and benefit) aloud until you sound relaxed and natural. When you think you have it perfected, ask a friend, co-worker, or family member to listen to your presentation. Ideally, choose someone who is not familiar with your product or service. If he or she can tell you exactly how a company will benefit from your offering, you will have mastered the concept. I will caution you—it sounds easier than it actually is.

THE POWER OF BODY LANGUAGE

"What you do speaks so loud that I cannot hear what you say."
Ralph Waldo Emerson

Much of what we say is communicated through our body language. And our nonverbal message is often more powerful than the words we use. Because of this, some experts suggest that you mirror the other person's body language. These experts state that this will help you more quickly connect with the person you are speaking to. However, unless you are well trained and highly skilled at using this technique, I believe that it will actually be more of a distraction.

The most important thing to remember is to relax, which can be challenging for several reasons:

- You may be unsure of the best way to start the conversation.

- You may be nervous.

- You might not be comfortable talking with executives.

- You may be concerned with closing the sale, especially if you have experienced a bit of a dry spell or slump.

- You may not be feeling well at the time.

Each of these can affect your body positioning, and thus the message you deliver to the other person. Lean back in your chair instead of leaning forward, and you will demonstrate a more relaxed body positioning.

Here are a few other pointers to keep in mind with respect to body language.

Arm crossing: Although you may naturally adopt this position, many people will perceive this as being defensive. When a customer or prospect is speaking, avoid crossing your arms, especially if the customer says something negative.

Fidgeting: This includes leg shaking or bouncing and foot tapping, which often indicate impatience or nervousness. Some people have a tendency to fidget when they are required to sit for long periods. However, exhibiting these movements during a client meeting will detract from your professionalism.

Yawning: This occurs when we are fatigued, drowsy, or bored. To prevent yawning during a meeting, I recommend that you drink plenty of water prior to your meeting. I have found that water refreshes my body and helps me overcome the natural fatigue that occurs during the day. Also, most people are more alert at certain times of day. Whenever possible, try to schedule important meetings when you have the most energy or are at your peak.

Stand: Always remain standing while waiting to meet a prospect. This helps eliminate the awkwardness you may experience trying to get up from a chair when your contact suddenly appears. Plus, this increases your energy level, which will be noticed by your prospect, client, or customer.

SALES TIP

Pay attention to the nonverbal message you deliver to your prospect or customer during your next sales call.

THE POWER OF CLARIFYING OBJECTIONS

"People don't always say what they are thinking."
Kelley Robertson

Objections are a natural part of the sale process. The most common objections include:

- "I'll think about it."

- "It's too expensive."

- "We don't have the budget."

- "We already have a supplier."

- "We're not interested."

- "We're talking to other vendors."

Clarifying a sales objection means restating the customer's comment back to them in your own words. The purpose of clarifying an objection is to ensure you have fully understood the customer's hesitation. Most salespeople incorrectly make the assumption they know what the objection is because they think they have heard the objection before. However, every customer is different, and although a customer may state an objection that may sound like one you have heard in the past, it could mean something entirely different.

For example, think of how often you hear customers say, "It's too expensive." If you are like most sales professionals you have probably heard this more times than you care to admit. Unfortunately, too many salespeople automatically think "it's too expensive" is a price objection and immediately offer a lower price. As a consumer and business owner, I have used this tactic simply to try to get a discount and I am constantly amazed how effective it is because the salesperson automatically assumed that I was not willing to pay the stated price. Just because a customer says "it's too expensive" does not mean that he or she is unwilling to pay the price. Let's take a closer look and see why the customer makes this statement:

- She does not see that value of your product or service.

- He cannot afford it.

- She is comparing your product to a similar product or service offered by another company.

- He is objecting as a negotiating tactic.

- She has not budgeted enough for it.

- His perception of the cost may be unrealistic.

- She is objecting as an excuse to not make the purchase.

- A competitor is selling the same product for less money.

Unless we clarify what the customer means, we will not likely be effective in overcoming the objection. If the customer does not see the value in your product or service you will need to take a different approach than if they are trying to negotiate a lower price. Yet most salespeople try to overcome the "it's too expensive" objection without first clarifying it. This is what clarifying the objection could sound like:

Customer:	"It's too expensive."
Salesperson:	"I can appreciate that; it is a significant investment. Would you mind telling me what you mean when you say that?"
Customer:	"I hadn't planned on spending that much money on this item."
Salesperson:	"I completely understand. You were planning to spend a certain amount and we've exceeded that budget, is that correct?"

Customer:	"Well, the real challenge is how I'm going to explain this to my boss so I can get the funding for it."
Salesperson:	"So it appears that you have a certain budget in mind and now you're just trying to figure out how to approach your manager so you can get the additional funding. Does that sound right?"
Customer:	"Yes."

In this last scenario, the original budget was the issue, but this underlying concern would not have risen to the surface had the salesperson not clarified the objection.

Many salespeople in my workshops initially think that the process of clarification takes too much time. My experience has taught me that it actually takes less time to deal with an objection, because you uncover the true objection much faster. This means that you can focus your "rebuttal" and address the real concern of your customer, thus spending less time offering solutions that are not relevant to that particular customer.

Another objection I hear is that it will sound condescending to restate the customer's objection to him. In actuality, it demonstrates that you have been listening to him and have heard his concern.

It's important to understand that very few people actually state their thoughts or what's on their mind. Let's say, for example, you sell software training and are talking to a new prospect about conducting a workshop for some of their employees. Here is how the dialogue might sound.

You:	"Would you like to go ahead and schedule a session for next month?"
Prospect:	"I'll think about it."
You:	"No problem. Most of my clients like to think about their decision before they move ahead. What particular concerns do you have?"
Prospect:	"I'm not sure this is the right thing for us right now."
You:	"I can appreciate that. Would you mind telling me what you mean by that?"

Prospect:	"We've done other software training before and found that it wasn't very relevant to our company."
You:	"I've heard other clients express the same concern before. Do you mind if I ask what happened in your situation?"
Prospect:	"The instructor read from a manual and a lot of people in the group already knew how to do what he was telling us. I got a lot of complaints from my staff afterward about how much time was wasted from their schedule."
You:	"I can definitely see why you are concerned. Your last session didn't address the specific issues and procedures your team wanted to learn so they got upset at you. It sounds like you are concerned that might happen again."
Prospect:	"That's right."

Imagine how this conversation could have gone had you not taken the time to learn exactly what concerns the prospect had. Yet, time and time again, salespeople hear that particular objection and respond with something like, "Okay, if you have any questions, give me a call," and then they leave or hang up the telephone. However, by helping the customer articulate her thoughts, you can learn exactly what her concern is.

SALES TIP

Invest the time to clarify your customer's objections until you uncover his true concern. Then you can respond with a solution that is appropriate to his specific situation instead of offering a solution that isn't relevant.

THE POWER OF CLARITY

"In order to achieve clarity and be fully and positively engaged in what you're doing, you must know the goal or outcome you're intending..."
David Allen, *Getting Things Done*

Having worked in the corporate world for over twenty years before striking out on my own, I was subjected to countless sales presentations. I noticed that most of the salespeople rambled during their presentation, particularly when they were nervous.

When I first began making sales calls I was surprised to find myself making the exact same mistake. I soon realized the reason: I did not have a clear message. It suddenly dawned on me that an effective sales presentation *must* be prepared ahead of time.

While I don't recommend the use of a scripted presentation, it is imperative to have a focused message. Instead of droning on about everything you and your company can offer a prospect, decide what key points you want to make. Write these points down and determine the most effective way to get your message across.

Executives are extremely busy. According to one source, it is estimated that the average business executive has less than one hour of unscheduled time in any given week. Plus, executives also have at least fifty hours of unfinished work on their desk at any given time.

Don't waste their time!

Know exactly what you want to say. Start with the most important point first. Keep your sentences as short as possible. Know how to get your message across *fast*! Practise key elements of your presentation. Record it so you can hear exactly what your prospect will hear. Time it so you know how long it takes to make each point. In today's fast-paced and highly competitive business world, you cannot afford to do otherwise.

SALES TIP

Focus your message. Know exactly what you want to say and how to say it. Get to the point. Clearly. And quickly. Watch how your client responds.

THE POWER OF COLD CALLING

"You have 10 seconds to succeed or fail."
Art Sobczak, *How to Sell More in Less Time with No Rejection*

I know very few people who actually enjoy cold calling—I know I certainly don't. However, it can be an effective way to generate leads and appointments when the right approach is used. Here are a few suggestions that can help improve the effectiveness of your cold calls.

Clearly identify the objective of each call. Do you want to arrange a face-to-face meeting or a telephone appointment? Are you trying to discover if the company has a need for your particular products or services? Are you using the call as a way to keep in touch with your prospect? The objective of your call will determine your approach and the introduction or message you leave.

Keep your introduction short and benefit-oriented. The majority of cold calls I receive as a business owner start with the salespeople rambling on about their company. Blah, blah, blah. Frankly, I don't care about who they work with, how long they have been in business, or what they do. I want to know how they can help me solve the problems I am currently experiencing in my business. Here is an example of the wrong approach:

"Hi Mr. Smith, it's Kelley calling from ACME Lawn Care. We have been in business since 1992 and we offer a wide variety of lawn care services.

We're going to be in your neighborhood next week. Would it be okay if we dropped by to give you a free estimate?"

The home owner will know that the objective of the "free estimate" is to sell lawn care services. However, most people will not see what's in it for them, which means they will probably decline the offer. Here is a more effective approach:

"Hi Mr. Smith, it's Pat calling from ACME Lawn Care. We specialize in helping small business owners such as yourself free up their time so they can focus on more important activities. We do this by providing a variety of lawn care services for you, which means you no longer have to spend your valuable time on things like weeding a garden, cutting your grass, or raking leaves. Can we set up a time to discuss this with you?"

Notice how this approach focuses on the customer instead of the supplier. It quickly demonstrates what the company does, but in terms that the customer can relate to. While it is not guaranteed to work in every situation, it will be effective because it focuses on benefits. I have discovered that most salespeople automatically think people will understand the benefits of their products and services. However, experience has taught me that we *must* clearly state these benefits to people to ensure they fully understand what's in it for them.

SALES TIP

Review Secret #11—The Power of Benefits and construct a telephone message that outlines or identifies one or more of the benefits of your products and services. Make sure your message focuses on the customer, not you or your business.

THE POWER OF CONFERENCES & TRADE SHOWS

"People at a booth can make or break business relationships."
Susan Friedmann, *The TradeShow Coach*

Conferences and trade shows can be an excellent way to meet new prospects, and many salespeople attend the events that are relevant to their industry. However, the key to boosting your sales is to seek out the conferences that your prospects attend.

Many of my clients are retailers so I attend retail-related conferences, trade shows, and networking events. I set a goal of introducing myself to a few decision-makers during the event but do not try to meet too many people. Instead, I focus on making a quality connection and invest my time learning as much about the contact's individual business as possible. After the conference, I send useful information to my new contacts on a regular basis. This approach has generated tens of thousands of dollars in sales, and it can work for you.

The best strategy is to identify the types of events that your ideal client would attend. You can start by asking existing customers what conferences they usually attend. Use the Internet to find out what conferences, trade shows, and events are scheduled in your local trading area and begin attending a few of them.

Another approach is to work a trade show with someone who is already connected in the industry. For example, I have worked one of my clients' booths so he could offer an additional service to his customers, spending most of my time answering sales-related questions for the people who visited the booth. I connected with new prospects and businesses and generated several qualified leads that eventually turned into business. I also took the same approach with a magazine I write for. The only cost I incurred was my time and I developed several new contacts.

If you decide to set up a booth at a trade show, avoid some of the common mistakes such as:

- eating food or chewing gum in your booth
- standing with your hands in your pockets
- trying to sell something to everyone who passes by
- relying solely on literature or glossy brochures to make the sale
- failing to follow up with qualified leads after the trade show

While trade shows may not be your cup of tea, visibility at the right one can yield great results, particularly if decision-makers of your target market attend.

You can also approach conferences and trade shows from a different perspective. Most events of this nature need people who can present information that will benefit their attendees. I know many people who have conducted breakout sessions at conferences and generated interest in their business as a result. A typical breakout session lasts approximately sixty to ninety minutes, and the best types of sessions are interactive. Here are a few tips to consider if you plan to use this strategy.

1. Start with a goal in mind. What information do you want attendees to leave with? Decide what key points would be most helpful and build your presentation around those points.

2. Too many breakout sessions feature a speaker who talks for the entire session. This means that the attendees are forced to listen rather than participate. If you want to stand out, find ways to involve your audience. You can achieve this by asking questions, creating discussion groups, or asking people to share their ideas.

3. Create high-quality handouts that include all of your contact information. These handouts should *not* be printouts of your slides or page upon page of text. Too many presenters simply print their PowerPoint slides in handout format. Don't think this approach separates them from the crowd. Instead, use bullet points, provocative questions, fill-in-the-blanks, and graphics. Whenever possible, I recommend printing these handouts on colored paper. This helps them stand out compared to materials that are printed on standard white paper. However, be aware that some conference planners will request that you submit your materials so they can be included in a conference binder.

4. Offer additional value to attendees by giving away an inexpensive product, consulting time, or other service you provide.

Once again, a word of caution; your presentation must deliver value to the conference attendees and *must not* be a blatant advertisement for your goods and services.

SALES TIP

Determine how trade shows or conferences could help your business. Identify the conferences or trade shows you should attend and establish an objective for each.

THE POWER OF CONFIDENCE

*"The best way to gain self-confidence
is to do what you are afraid to do."*

People want to buy from individuals who are confident in their abilities. Taking control of the circumstances and situations around you will develop your self-confidence. When you consider the amount of rejection that many salespeople encounter, the fact that many salespeople lack self-confidence is not surprising. Top-performing people in any industry typically possess a high level of self-confidence. They may not have possessed this confidence all their lives.

I have not always had a lot of self-confidence. Outwardly I was Mr. Confident while on the inside I seriously doubted my abilities. I had to wrestle with my own mental baggage for years before I became internally confident. Learning to be confident begins with letting go of your personal baggage.

Mental baggage is a collection of *all* the situations we have experienced or encountered during our lifetimes. We carry all this baggage around in our heads and draw from it when appropriate situations present themselves. Perhaps you tried to join a school sports team when you were a child. Your athletic abilities in that particular sport were average; for that reason you were unable to make the team. You filed away this experience in your subconscious until a similar situation came along. You immediately recalled the previous performance and outcome, and told yourself that you were not capable of successfully meeting the current challenge. Consequently, you did not make the effort required to meet it.

We all carry around this mental baggage. It influences everything we do, in both our business and personal lives. How it affects us when we sell is very simple. Mental baggage may consist of customers who have been rude, abrupt, or angry toward us. Baggage can include situations from earlier in our work careers or even from our childhoods.

As time progresses, this mental baggage weighs heavier and heavier. Yet we continue to drag it around with us into every sales situation. Over time our attitude turns sour, we become pessimistic and jaded, and we get frustrated with challenging customers and prospects. Our productivity drops, our performance slides, and our job security may even be threatened. We become increasingly bitter toward our chosen occupation, the customers we serve, and life in general.

How do we prevent this from happening? First, carrying around mental baggage is a natural part of being human. It is the way we view and deal with our baggage that makes the real difference in our lives. If we look at each experience and consider how we can learn from it, our baggage will have less hold over us. I recall the first paid keynote presentation I gave. I was well prepared, but not in the appropriate manner. The room was an awkward shape and the stage was positioned quite high, something I had never dealt with previously. I was uncomfortable during my presentation and I knew my delivery was affected. Instead of focusing on this after my session, I chose to concentrate on what I learned from the experience.

Second we must understand that every sales situation is completely different than the others we've experienced. Even though you may be prepared for your sales meeting, something completely unexpected may arise, which could affect your ability to make a great presentation. However, as time progresses and you encounter more situations, you will develop the confidence to effectively deal with new situations. The key is to realize that you will learn from every sales conversation. Third, we must recognize that some of our baggage is outdated. We may be relying on information that is several years old. This happened to me at the beginning of my career.

When I was twenty-three I was working for a restaurant chain as an assistant manager. I was promoted to general manager and lasted less than a year before I was demoted back to an assistant manager. I had proved unable to perform to the company's expectations. I ended up leaving the company shortly afterward. For five years I hesitated any time an opportunity for a promotion presented itself; I had not been sure I could do it. Finally it dawned on me exactly what I had learned from that earlier experience. I was not the only person responsible for that particular failure, and my leadership and managerial skills had developed since then. Nevertheless, it took me five years to realize it! Let go of your mental baggage and work on developing your personal confidence.

SALES TIP

Develop your personal confidence by creating a list of your strengths, and identify how each of these strengths contributes to your sales success. Review this list on a regular basis to give yourself a continual boost. If you are unsure of your strengths, ask close friends or business associates for their opinion. One word of caution: make sure you ask someone who will be honest and open with you and whose feedback you trust.

THE POWER OF COURAGE

*"Courage is not the absence of fear or lack of fear.
It is control of fear, mastery of fear."*
Mark Twain

Virtually every salesperson experiences some form of fear during his or her career. Whether it is selling to a large account, dealing with an irate customer, delivering a presentation to a new prospect, or cold calling, it takes courage to become successful at selling.

It is okay to feel anxiety and concern when faced with a new project or something you haven't tried before. However, the difference between winners and everyone else is that winners have developed the courage to push beyond their personal comfort zone.

A friend of mine is deathly afraid of flying and during one particular business trip he found himself in a position where he was required to fly by helicopter. He told me later that he was terrified but he knew his only options were to cancel the trip and forfeit the fee he had been paid or to make the trip. He faced his fear and took the helicopter ride. Although he admitted to being scared during the flight, he felt exhilarated when he landed knowing that he faced his fear and survived.

I once read the definition of fear as being "False Expectations Appearing Real." In all but a few situations, the concerns that cause us the most grief or fear seldom become reality. The best way to deal with fear is to confront it. As Susan Jeffers penned, "Feel the fear, do it anyway." The more often you do these things, the more quickly you will develop the confidence and courage to continue.

SALES TIP

Identify the aspects of your job or business that cause you stress or anxiety. Select one of these and determine what action you are prepared to take. Then set a deadline for taking this action.

THE POWER OF CREDIBILITY

"In the end, you make your reputation and you have your success based upon credibility."
Brit Hume

Always, always, always be honest. I once read that if you always tell the truth you never have to remember what you said. This quote struck a chord with me because I have worked with, and have seen, too many salespeople who stretch the truth or deliberately lie in order to close a sale. What's even worse is the way salespeople try to justify this behavior. Is it any wonder customers are skeptical when they talk to a salesperson?

Here are a few things you can do to increase your credibility with new prospects and existing customers.

Listen more than you talk. Most salespeople I know talk far too much and dominate conversations with prospects. The most successful ones I know invest more time listening and less time talking. See Secret #50—The Power of Listening for more ideas on this topic.

Deliver on your promises. We have all heard the expression, "under-promise and over-deliver." This may be a simple concept in theory, but it is a very challenging principle in reality. If you make a commitment to a customer, do everything in your power to deliver on that promise. From phone calls to delivery times, everything you do affects your credibility in your customer's mind.

If it feels wrong, don't do it. We are all faced with situations that do not feel right. However, in many cases, we forge ahead and close the deal. I remember a conversation with a prospect a few years ago. As the discussion progressed, I felt uncomfortable about the derogatory way he talked about his sales team. I ignored these feelings, eventually closed the sale, and later conducted the training program we had discussed. When I followed up with my customer a few weeks after the program I was disappointed—but not surprised—to learn that his team had not adjusted their sales approach. I knew my customer had wasted his money and I felt badly because I could have prevented it. At that point, I made a conscious decision to *never* accept an assignment just for the sake of closing another sale.

Refer a competitor. Sometimes it makes sense to refer a prospect to a competitor. When I think of this concept, I am always reminded of the Christmas movie *Miracle on 34th Street* when the real Santa Claus tells a customer that she should shop at the competition because his store is out of stock of a particular item. You cannot be everything to everybody. But most salespeople would rather sell something their customer does not need, or want than lose a sale to a competitor.

Make your customer comfortable. The majority of people experience some level of discomfort when dealing with a salesperson. You can reduce this discomfort by focusing on helping your customer rather than closing the sale. You can also tell a prospect that it is okay to say no at any time during the sales process.

Ultimately, you, and you alone are responsible for the level of credibility you develop with your prospects and customers.

SALES TIP

Decide what you can do to improve your credibility with your clients and prospects. This may take some serious self-evaluation, but in the end it will be worthwhile. For instance, some people set unrealistic time frames for the completion of a project, which means they fail to meet the scheduled deadline. They could improve their credibility by establishing a later deadline. This would allow them more time to complete the project, and if they finished the project ahead of schedule, would demonstrate their reliability.

THE POWER OF CUSTOMER SERVICE

"Customers don't expect you to be perfect.
They do expect you to fix things when they go wrong."
Donald Porter

Although customer service may not official-
ly be in your title or job description, top sales
professionals know that delivering outstanding customer service
will help them maintain a competitive advantage. In many cases you
are the primary link between your customer and your company. That
means it is up to you to ensure that your customer receives the service
he or she expects. As a consumer and business owner, I am very particular about who gets my business. I no longer give my hard-earned money
to people who fail to deliver good service. I prefer to buy from companies
who offer excellent service, but this is becoming more and more difficult
all the time.

Very few salespeople actually deliver excellent service. Certainly the
policies and procedures of their company limit them to a certain degree.
But in many situations, the customer-service issues are caused by the
salespeople themselves. Selling something that is on back order, making
a commitment that is next to impossible to keep, or failing to follow up
as promised are all too common in the sales environment.

However, here are a few key strategies that can help you deliver great service:

1. **Ask your customers what they expect.** One of the challenges with this concept is that every customer has different expectations. Your goal is to determine what those expectations are and work at exceeding them. This may sound simple, but experience has taught me that few people excel at this concept. But what better way to learn how best to approach them? For example, if a web designer were to ask me what was important to me with respect to service, my automatic answer would be, "Tell me when the changes I request are completed and respond to my e-mail and voice mail messages within twenty-four hours."

2. **Apologize when you make a mistake.** We addressed this concept in Secret #3. It constantly surprises me how few businesses actually make the effort to apologize when they make a mistake.

3. **Put yourself in your customer's position.** What would you expect if a similar situation happened to you? What type of response would you deem necessary? How would you like the problem handled?

4. **Avoid saying, "That's our policy."** We all know that policies exist to protect the organization, and the larger the company, the bigger the policy and procedure manual is. But customers don't care about your policies and procedures. They want their problem rectified. And they want it done now!

5. **Make it easy for people to do business with you.** Don't make people jump through hoops to resolve a situation. I can think of dozens of situations when I have expressed a problem to a salesperson or customer-service rep only to be challenged on the cause of the problem.

6. **Respond quickly.** In today's business world, it is imperative to respond to calls and requests for information *fast*. The voice-mail

message of a business associate of mine states that he will return calls within four hours. And he consistently delivers on this promise. It is little wonder his business continues to grow in leaps and bounds. One of my service standards is to respond to all e-mail correspondence within twenty-four hours unless I happen to be traveling and do not have access to e-mail. It often means I spend more time at my computer than I prefer, but I receive many comments from my clients and business associates that indicate their surprise and delight at this quick response.

Delivering great customer service does not have to be difficult. But it starts with a mindset and a commitment.

SALES TIP

Look at your business from a customer's perspective. Listen to the complaints or concerns you receive and take action to correct these shortcomings, particularly if you hear the same concern repeatedly. When you encounter a negative customer-service situation with another business, ask yourself if you are guilty of making the same or similar mistakes in your business.

THE POWER OF DETAILS

"The difference between something good and something great is attention to detail."
Charles R. Swindoll

Richard Carlson wrote a book called *Don't Sweat the Small Stuff.* But details are crucial in sales. It is the small stuff that can make a difference in our level of success.

- It means knowing your customer's preferences, likes, and dislikes.

- It is spelling the customer's name correctly.

- It is listening carefully to the customer so you can determine the best course of action or solution.

- It means thinking of the implications of the solution in all areas of your customer's business.

- It means carefully reading any contract and making sure your work is error-free, including spelling and grammar in your e-mail correspondence.

- It includes recording the details of your conversations so you can adapt your approach and refer to these details later in the sales process.

- It means seeking clarification when you are uncertain what a customer means.

- It means communicating with prospects via their preferred method (e-mail, telephone, face-to-face).

- It is following through on your commitments—when you say you will.

- It includes being on time for meetings, phone calls, and sales appointments.

- It includes sending thank-you cards and letters.

Details are the bane of many businesses. It is simple to take care of the "big stuff" but the details can be missed or forgotten and can quickly bog you down. You may rely on other people in your company to help you with some of these, but it is still your responsibility to make sure the work gets done. Pay attention to the details in your business, and the business will take care of you.

SALES TIP

What details do you need to take care of? What can you do to ensure they are completed? Here is an example:

I review a checklist before each workshop, speech, or session even though I have been delivering some of my programs for many years. This ensures that I don't forget anything for that particular workshop, speech, or session.

Another example could be to use the spell-check feature in your software to ensure your spelling, grammar, and punctuation are accurate.

THE POWER OF DISCIPLINE

"A journey of a thousand miles begins with a single step."

One of the characteristics that separates most successful salespeople from everyone else is discipline. According to *Webster's Dictionary*, discipline is defined as "controlled behavior resulting from training; self-control."

Discipline in sales means:

- Starting early and finishing late. As Ken Blanchard once said, "To be successful, all you have to do is work half-days; you can work the first twelve hours or the second twelve." I'm not suggesting that you have to work sixty hours a week, every week. However, the more effort you put into your business, the better your results will be.

- Making calls even when you do not feel like it. The vast majority of salespeople do not discipline themselves to make a certain number of calls each and every day and week, especially when they are tired or not feeling well. Top sales performers make their calls regardless of how they feel.

- Practising your presentation one more time. This often-neglected aspect of selling is critical. I remember watching a friend introduce a speaker at an industry conference. The entire presentation was less than five minutes in length, but Tim invested almost two hours practising it the night before. See Secret #67—The Power of Preparation and Secret #68—The Power of Presentations for more information on this topic.

- Investing more time learning about your products. A cursory review of your products is not sufficient in today's ultracompetitive marketplace. If you want to stand out, you need to invest time learning everything there is to know about your products.

- Thoroughly researching your prospects before contacting them. Too many executives receive unsolicited calls from salespeople who have not done adequate research and expect the executive to give them information that could have been uncovered in their annual report or web site or by talking to an employee or customer of that company.

So how can you develop this discipline? It starts with a conscious decision and desire to succeed. I once read a quote from a Detroit Pistons player: "To be great you can't cut corners. Natural skills are fine, but hard work makes you a champion." Decide now that you will do what it takes to reach the level of success you desire. You will find that your mental focus will shift the instant you make this decision.

SALES TIP

When you find yourself putting off a task, repeat to yourself, "Do it now, do it now, do it now." This mantra will force you to do the task, which is the first step to beating procrastination and developing your personal discipline.

THE POWER OF EFFECTIVE INTRODUCTIONS

"Do you suppose I could buy back my introduction to you?"
Groucho Marx

Can you describe what you do in thirty seconds or less? Successful salespeople can accurately describe what they sell and to whom in a few short, concise sentences. This may sound easy, but the majority of people have a difficult time explaining what they do. This is particularly true for individuals who sell a service rather than a tangible product. I recall attending a networking event and speaking with the owner of a small business who could not articulate what she did. After a twenty-minute conversation and after I asked her several questions, I still was unsure what her exact business was. You can imagine how difficult it would be for me to refer business to this individual, not knowing exactly what she did.

There are several ways to create an effective introduction. You can start with a question and, when the other person responds, you elaborate on the services you provide. Here is an example:

"Do you ever wish your sales team would ask for the sale more consistently?" Assuming the answer is yes, you could respond with, "I work with sales teams to help them become more confident in asking for the sale."

Your next step is to identify your ideal client or target market. "I work with Fortune 500 companies who have a sales force of at least twenty-five people."

One of the keys is to adapt your introduction to make sure it relates to the person you are speaking with.

Another approach is to simply state what you do as well as one the benefits of your services. For example, "I work with entrepreneurs to help them increase the effectiveness of their web sites. I focus on helping them optimize their web site, which translates into more revenue for them."

Still another approach is to start with what you do, then add an example of or story about the results you have achieved. Here is what this approach would sound like: "I work with retailers to help them sell more accessories and add-on items. One of my clients experienced a nineteen-point eight percent increase in add-on sales after implementing the concepts I suggested."

Your goal is to develop an introduction that piques the other person's interest and will cause him to ask questions about what you do. This is especially true if you have allowed him to talk about himself and his business. This then gives you the chance to discuss your business and explore potential sales opportunities.

I remember when I first started my own business. When I was asked what I did, I usually responded with something like, "I'm a sales trainer."

I'll be the first to admit that this is not a very intriguing introduction. Even though I knew my introduction could be better, I did not work on perfecting it for quite some time. And in the beginning, I changed it every time I stated it. This prevented me from becoming comfortable and confident using my introduction. I learned that practising my introduction was as important as the introduction itself. This does not mean running it through your head a few times before a networking event. It means stating it so often that you can recite it automatically in virtually any type of networking event or situation.

SALES TIP

If you don't have a standard introduction, take the time now to create one. Practise saying it until it flows smoothly and without hesitation.

THE POWER OF ELEVATOR SPEECHES

"Success is where preparation and opportunity meet."
Bobby Unser

Imagine finding yourself alone with a key prospect in an elevator. Before you reach the end of your ride would you be prepared to tell her what you do and how you can help her company? Most salespeople can't. That is why it is important to develop an elevator speech. Although you may never be faced with this particular situation, you must be ready to talk about your business— quickly and concisely.

An elevator speech is similar to an effective introduction except that it is a bit longer, about sixty seconds compared to a twenty- or thirty-second introduction. The objective is to introduce yourself and your company to your prospect and give her an idea of the results she can achieve with your product or service.

Your elevator speech should contain a story of how your product or service has helped someone. It should also be structured so that it piques the other person's interest enough to ask you for more information.

Like a short introduction, it must be practised. It is essential that this presentation is so well rehearsed that you can recite it in your sleep. However, it should not sound like a sales pitch, which means you need to ensure that your tone and delivery are smooth, confident, and conversational. This will ensure that the elevator speech comes across as natural, genuine, and sincere.

SALES TIP

Take your standard introduction and add an example or story of how you helped a particular client or company. Focus on results you can help the other person achieve. Like your introduction, take time to practise verbalizing it so you can recite it easily and naturally when necessary.

THE POWER OF ELIMINATING FINE PRINT

"Nothing in fine print is ever good news."
Andy Rooney

A lease for some office equipment came due after three years. Neither my wife nor I could recall the exact date the lease expired, but I expected the leasing company to notify me. Unfortunately, they did not. This meant that I continued making payments on a product I was ready to replace. When I questioned the company on their policy I was bluntly told that my contract stated that it was *my* responsibility to contact them upon the expiration of my lease. Technically, it was my mistake. I did not read all the fine print in the multipage contract.

However, from a sales and customer service point of view, they could have managed the situation much better. How difficult would it be for them to tell a new customer of this policy upon acceptance of the contract? A simple step that I'm sure would eliminate many customer complaints and frustration later on.

We know that the fine print in a contract is meant to protect the company and reduce its liability. However, it's how we manage the fine print that makes the difference. Not advising customers about details, limitations, and responsibilities is no different than deliberately misleading them in an effort to get their business.

What fine print do you have in your contracts? What terms do you hide from your customers? Do you clearly explain the conditions of doing business with your company? Do you make the terms and conditions of that particular purchase readily available to every customer and client? Or do you surprise them afterward?

An executive at a meeting I attended stated that the more conditions you place on a person's purchase (business or personal), the more difficult you make it for the customer to do business with you. Ultimately, the less fine print you have, the easier you make it for someone to do business with you, and the more you will profit.

SALES TIP

Review the fine print in your contracts and look for ways to reduce or eliminate as much of it as possible. You can also point out the fine print to your customers in advance so they are aware of it, which will also help you develop more credibility.

THE POWER OF
E-MAIL

"Get a real email address. None of this hotmail or AOL crap."
Jeffrey Gitomer, *The Sales Bible*

E-mail is an awesome sales tool—when it is used properly. Most of the sales professionals and small business owners I talk to can't figure out why buyers or prospects do not respond to their e-mail messages. Here is a fact of business—the average executive receives in excess of 150 e-mail messages. Every day! It is little wonder the buyer of the company you are trying to connect with does not send you a prompt reply.

Here are a few key points to remember:

- Use a powerful or strong subject line. Too many e-mail messages are vague and meaningless to the recipient. If you want to capture your prospect's attention, the subject line must compel her to open your message.

- If you plan to send the same e-mail to multiple people, do not use the cc feature, because it exposes each person's e-mail address to everyone on the list. With the amount of spam generated today, I like to guard my e-mail address and those of my clients. Use the bcc feature for the people you wish to copy on the message.

- Think before you send. Double-check your message. Ensure that the spelling and punctuation are correct, that all the information is included, and that any attachments are actually attached. I can't count the number of times I have sent an e-mail in haste only to forget the attachment. This costs you and your prospect time. And time is money!

- Avoid sending complex or complicated information. In this case, it is usually more effective to call your customer and talk to her.

- Do not expect a response. I recently heard that up to forty percent of e-mail messages are never received. If you are sending vital information, it may be better to call your prospect and leave a voice-mail message advising him of your intentions.

If you use e-mail to sell your product or service, I suggest the following strategies:

- Do not send too many messages. Some marketers send out several e-mails to each client every week hoping to generate sales. If you want to be effective, avoid inundating people. Otherwise, your messages will quickly end up in the trash can. Send your customers and prospects useful information, for example, articles that will help your clients improve their business. A friend of mine subscribes to several different newsletters and when she comes across something that she thinks will benefit her customers, she forwards it to them. Once again, do not go overboard with this. An article or a link to web site once a month is sufficient.

- One of the most effective e-mail strategies is to create your own newsletter. I write a weekly newsletter called *The 59 Second Sales Tip* and it has generated thousands of dollars in sales. More information on this topic can be found in Secret #54—The Power of Newsletters.

- If you use e-mail to initiate contact with a prospect, keep it brief and avoid "pitching" your business. Instead, focus on explaining the benefits of your product or service. Do your research and adapt your message to each prospective client. Also, make sure you include a day and time when you will follow up by telephone.

SALES TIP

Evaluate the e-mails that you send to customers and prospects. Put yourself in their position and ask yourself what you would think if you were on the receiving end of that e-mail. Is each e-mail message necessary? Do you keep them concise and to the point? Does the subject line give the recipient a clear idea of what you want? Do you include a call-to-action and deadlines when appropriate?

THE POWER OF EMOTIONS

"Let's not forget that the little emotions are the great captains of our lives and we obey them without realizing it."
Vincent Van Gogh

According to Pamela Danziger, author of *Why People Buy Things They Don't Need*, people buy things they don't need to achieve emotional comfort. Emotional comfort for consumers may include having the latest technology, gadget or "toy," the fun of being one of the first to see a particular movie, or the status of being able to afford a luxury item. On the corporate side, emotional comfort could include saving money for the organization, negotiating a great deal, or looking good in front of peers or supervisors.

A very successful sales coach I know asks all prospects to complete a brief questionnaire when they first contact him. He follows this with a series of well-thought-out questions that explore the depth of his prospect's situation. As he delves deeper into their business concerns, the prospects begin to get more emotionally connected with the issue or problem. They start to see the severity of the problem. They often realize the financial impact the current situation will have on the business. As they become more emotionally involved in the sales process, price becomes less of an issue. As a result, the sales coach usually generates much more business than the one or two days of sales training or coaching the company originally contacted him about.

Increasing a person's emotional quotient in the sales process also means delivering an engaging sales presentation. Using descriptive words—adjectives and adverbs—and painting mental images in your presentation are just a few ways to create this emotional connection. In some of my training workshops I encourage participants to create a list of descriptive words that will enhance their presentation. I recall listening to one salesperson after the workshop use the phrase, "Imagine what this will look like in your living room when you take it home." The customer responded positively because he could visualize himself using the product.

You can also actively involve your customers in the presentation instead of forcing them to be passive bystanders. Whenever possible, have samples for them to see. People are tactile creatures and need to touch and feel products. This can help to create a connection between your product and your prospective customers.

If you sell a professional service, it may be difficult to show specific examples of your work. Consider videotaping or capturing photos of you interacting with clients. Create a binder of testimonials, or better yet, have some of your clients express their thoughts about your service verbally as a digital recording. I have seen many web sites that use verbal testimonials as well as written.

The more emotionally connected people feel with your product or service, the greater the likelihood they will buy from you.

SALES TIP

Identify the emotional reasons people buy your product or service and determine the best way you can express these reasons to future prospects.

THE POWER OF EMPATHY

"Some people think only intellect counts: knowing how to solve problems, knowing how to get by, knowing how to identify an advantage and seize it. But the functions of intellect are insufficient without empathy."

Dean Koontz

Empathy means putting yourself in the other person's position. This is a great sales tool because it can change the dynamics of the interaction between the salesperson and the customer. Many salespeople mentally empathize with their customers. Unfortunately, this is not enough. You need to express empathy aloud to your customers. Putting empathy into words shows your customers that you care, that you are on their side, that you understand, respect, or appreciate them. Most people want others to empathize with them and their situation. When I first began running I experienced shin splints. Shin splints are a very painful injury often caused by worn-out shoes. While I was replacing my shoes I began telling the sales associate about my injury so she could fully understand what I needed.

Empathy can be used very effectively in service issues. Consider the customer who is returning a defective product. He is often upset, angry, frustrated. When he begins his attack, the service worker's first reaction is to retaliate with a comment like, "I just sell them, I don't make them," or, "Yeah, we get this model returned a lot." Such comments only fuel the customer's already heated emotions. It is more advantageous to empathize with him in a situation like this. "You have every right to be upset; I'd feel the same way too. Let me see what I can do to help."

Empathy helps diffuse the situation. It helps reduce the customer's hostility, and it helps you move toward a solution. A few years ago I received a parking ticket. On reading it carefully, I noticed that the street name was incorrectly recorded. I drove to the city finance office to discuss the error. When the clerk enquired whether I was disputing the ticket, I said yes. She responded, "If you want to dispute the ticket you'll have to show up in court." As I continued to question her, she kept repeating this. No matter what I said, she repeated the same thing over and over. Needless to say, my level of frustration escalated dramatically. Surely she could have told me, "I can appreciate your frustration, Mr. Robertson. Unfortunately, my hands are tied. In situations like this, it's your word against the parking officer's so the matter has to be handled in court." If she had said this along with some words of genuine empathy I probably would have paid the ten-dollar fine and been on my way.

There are many ways to phrase an expression of empathy:

- "I understand how you feel."
- "I appreciate your concern."
- "I respect your decision."
- "I see why you feel that way."
- "I've been there so I know how you feel."
- "You're right; it is a major investment."
- "You're not alone; other people have said the same thing."
- "That's not the first time I've heard that."
- "I hear what you're saying."
- "I see what you mean."

Each of these statements demonstrates your understanding of the customer's perspective. You can adapt these statements to each customer you deal with and the specific objection he or she presents.

SALES TIP

Practise using a variety of the empathy statements listed in this chapter. If, during your next sales call, your prospect or customer expresses any form of concern, use the most appropriate statement for that particular situation.

THE POWER OF ENGAGING YOUR CUSTOMER

"Engage me and you can make me convince myself."
Jeffrey Gitomer, *Little Red Book of Selling*

A fully engaged customer will express fewer objections. A customer who is engaged in the sales process will be more likely to buy from you. An engaged customer will spend more money. Doesn't it make sense to make sure your customers are fully and actively involved in the sales interaction?

Unfortunately, most salespeople spend time talking and trying to figure out how they can sell their product or service, instead of focusing on how they can involve their customer.

Here are three simple strategies you can use that will help with this.

- **Ask customers more questions.** This helps get them involved in the sales process and will engage them. Many people like to hear the sound of their own voice and will gladly respond to questions. Make sure the questions are relevant to the customer's situation.

- **Listen more than you talk.** While many salespeople think that telling is selling, you can actually increase your sales by giving your customers more airtime.

- **If you sell a product, encourage the customers to touch, feel, and operate it.** The more emotionally connected customers are with the product, the more likely they will buy it. Most salespeople *tell* their customers how something works, but very few actually allow the customers to operate it.

Engaging customers is not that difficult. But it does require a selfless approach. This means that you need to be more focused on the customers' needs and situation than on closing the sale.

SALES TIP

Identify specific ways you can more actively engage your customers in the sales process. As you experiment with these approaches, watch how people respond to you.

THE POWER OF ENTHUSIASM

*"For every sale you miss because you're too enthusiastic,
you will miss a hundred because you're not enthusiastic enough."*
Zig Ziglar

Our personal enthusiasm has a tremendous impact on our clientele and our ability to close sales.
If we simply go through the motions, ask prospective clients just a few
questions when we qualify them, present the product in a lackluster fashion, and become defensive when clients toss us objections, we can reason-
ably expect the customers will not be motivated to buy.

On the other hand, if we maintain an enthusiastic behavior it will
shine through when we're talking to that person. If we get excited when
we explain our product or service, the customer will get excited too. If
we smile and use some humor during the sale, the client will relax and
open up. All of this adds up to one thing: more sales.

Most of the sales presentations I hear as a consumer, business owner,
and sales trainer are dull and boring. Your words, tone of voice, and body
language must convey your interest and desire. Your choice of words and
how you express yourself greatly influence your customer's buying decision. You must believe in your product. You must think or, better yet,
know that your service offers tremendous benefits.

Being "on" is a critical success factor in sales. You need to be on and
demonstrate to customers why they should buy from you. If you're

not excited and enthusiastic about what you do you will not be able to convince customers to buy from you instead of a competitor.

While this may sound simple in theory, the ability to remain enthusiastic can be difficult, especially during dry spells. Here are a few techniques that can help you maintain a high level of enthusiasm.

- First of all, you must believe in your product or service. Many people lose their enthusiasm after they have been selling a particular product for a period of time. Take the time to review how your product or service benefits your customers. Look for unique characteristics that your product offers.

- Talk to existing customers who are happy with your product and listen to their positive comments.

- Enthusiasm is contagious and one of the most effective ways to stay enthusiastic is to associate with positive and enthusiastic people.

- Read or listen to motivational material or inspiring stories.

Behavior is contagious; is yours worth catching?

SALES TIP

One of the most enlightening exercises you can do is to record several of your presentations. Listen with a critical ear to how you sound when speaking to a client. If this option is not suitable to your business, ask a friend to listen to your presentation. Ask for honest feedback and incorporate her advice into your next presentation.

THE POWER OF EXERCISE

"In general, any form of exercise, if pursued continuously, will help train us in perseverance."
Mao Tse-Tung

Exercise creates energy. It can help us focus. It can generate the mental sharpness we need to close a sale. I trained for my first marathon (26.2 miles) in 1998, and at the peak of my training, my mental focus was sharper than I had ever experienced. I learned that regular exercise creates endorphins. Endorphins create energy. And energy helps the brain work more effectively.

Many of the most successful people in the world exercise regularly even though their schedules run into sixteen- and eighteen-hour days. There is a direct correlation between fitness and success. While it may not be politically correct, few obese and out-of-shape people become truly successful. The reason is simple: success takes effort, energy, and stamina.

I have experienced weight loss and gain. I have been at my ideal weight and I know what it feels like to be thirty pounds overweight. I know the feeling of running forty-five miles a week and I also know the feeling of being a couch potato. And I know from experience that engaging in regular exercise helps me increase my sales and revenues.

Regular exercise not only makes you mentally sharper and more focused, it also gives you the opportunity to think about your business challenges. This personal time gives your brain time to think about and process during recent sales conversations. When I was running, I often came up with new ideas and solutions and a friend of mine frequently rehearses upcoming presentations during his jogs.

Something as simple as a fifteen-to-twenty-minute walk in the morning or evening can do wonders to improve your energy. Even stretching on a daily basis can improve your circulation and give you more energy.

SALES TIP

Make a commitment to engage in some form of regular activity or exercise at least three to four times a week. It will take a few weeks for the results of your efforts to kick in, but before long you will notice an increase in your mental sharpness and your physical energy. This improvement will quickly transfer itself to your sales results.

THE POWER OF FACE-TO-FACE MEETINGS

"When I was a graduate student at Harvard, I learned about showers and central heating. Ten years later, I learned about breakfast meetings. These are America's three great contributions to civilization."
Mervyn A. King

Telephones and e-mail certainly save sales professionals time. In fact, it is not uncommon to close sales using only these tools. However, I firmly believe that the face-to-face meeting is still one of the most effective ways to close a sale. I find that a face-to-face meeting allows for a better exchange of information—from both parties.

Sitting across a desk or boardroom table from a prospective customer gives me the opportunity to better connect with him. I can watch his body language, notice nuances in his facial expressions, and pick up clues from his office that might help me close the sale.

Certainly, in some situations, a face-to-face meeting is not always possible. I also know several people who try to avoid face-to-face meetings to save time. While I don't disagree with them, I do believe that a personal meeting allows you to "strut your stuff" more effectively. A sales trainer friend of mine uses face-to-face meetings to demonstrate his "front-of-the-room" delivery skills. He often stands up and uses the chalkboard, whiteboard, or flip chart to reinforce his key points.

Preparation is critical for a face-to-face meeting. Each meeting has a different objective. This means you need to take a different approach when preparing.

If you are meeting a prospect for the first time you may need to invest a few minutes talking about your business and highlighting some of your success. Note that I said *a few minutes*. This does not mean you spend half an hour droning on and on and on. Be prepared to give a high-level overview of your organization then focus the rest of the meeting on your prospect, learning more about her specific situation and how you might be able to help her.

If this is a second meeting—to discuss a proposal, possible solutions, and so on—I recommend you start with a brief summary or recap of the previous meeting. Most executives and corporate buyers meet with many salespeople. Although the details of the meeting are likely fresh in your mind, the prospect will seldom recall what you talked about. Summarizing your last meeting will help refresh her memory.

Once the summary is complete, you should begin your sales presentation. However, avoid falling into the trap of talking at great length, unless this is a formal presentation. During a sales appointment with a particular existing client, I started the conversation by asking what type of program he wanted. The executive responded, "We have a few ideas. Why don't you tell me what you have in mind?" For many salespeople this would be an open path to present their ideas. However, I wanted to make sure that I was on the right track, so I presented one of the several ideas I had and then asked, "How does that compare with what you were thinking about?" He then started telling me what he and his coworker had talked about.

During a face-to-face meeting, you must pay attention to your appearance. My personal belief is that you should dress one step higher than your prospect does. It is always easier to downgrade your appearance than to upgrade it. If you show up wearing a suit and tie but your prospect is only wearing casual pants and golf shirt, you can take off the jacket, loosen your tie, and roll up your sleeves. However, if you dress in a casual manner but your contact arrives in a suit and tie, there isn't much you can do to improve your appearance.

When you schedule a face-to-face meeting, make sure you bring all necessary items to deliver a great presentation. Even though you may not need everything, it is better to show up prepared and ready to go.

SALES TIP

Identify what you can do to improve the quality and impact of your face-to-face meetings. If you have several items on this list, determine which one will have the greatest immediate impact and implement it first. Then continue the process with the remaining items on your list.

THE POWER OF FACIAL EXPRESSIONS

*"If I had to choose to focus on the body or the face—
I'd focus on the face."*
Robert Tracz, *Secrets of Face-to-Face Communication*

I have watched hundreds of salespeople when they interact with customers and have been constantly surprised at the lack of facial expressions many of them show when talking to potential customers.

Many seem to think that they must maintain a poker face. One salesperson admitted to me that he refrained from showing emotion because he was concerned that prospects would think he was too eager for the sale. Selling is not a poker game! Use your facial expressions to increase the impact of your communication. Show interest in what your customer says and respond accordingly.

People respond to the facial expressions you exhibit. That's why I make a point of smiling frequently when I'm speaking with my clients and prospects—unless, of course, the topic is a serious one.

Be aware of the facial expressions you show during your sales presentations. If you smile frequently during your presentation, your customer will smile also. This will make her more comfortable with you and help reduce the tension that people sometimes feel in some sales interactions. However, if you smile while making a serious point, you will lose credibility.

Facial expressions are also important when you are speaking to someone on the telephone. Many call center trainers suggest placing a mirror on your desk or on the wall in front you so you can see yourself while you are talking to people. It is surprising what we learn when we actually see our expressions.

SALES TIP

Determine what facial expressions you need to exhibit during specific situations. Practise using these expressions so you become comfortable with them *before* you meet with prospect, clients, and customers.

THE POWER OF FEEL, FELT, FOUND

"People don't care how much you know until they know how much you care."
Zig Ziglar

An effective way to deal with objections is to use the "feel, felt, found" method. Here is how it works.

When the customer expresses an objection, let's say, "That's a lot more than we budgeted," you respond with something like:

"I understand how you *feel*."

"Other people have *felt* the same way."

"What they have *found* is…"

This approach shows that you understand the customer's perspective. It demonstrates empathy and changes the dynamics of the sales process because it reduces the other person's defensiveness.

It tells your customer that other people have been in a similar situation or experienced the same thoughts or feelings. This, too, helps reduce defensiveness.

Finally, give an example of how a client solved a problem by using your product or service. The example demonstrates why your current client should buy from you.

What makes this approach so effective is that you have taken the time to demonstrate that you have actually listened to your customer. Remember, even if you have heard the same objection dozens or even hundreds of times before, your customers want their individual concerns to be taken seriously.

SALES TIP

List the most common objections you hear and create responses for each of them using the "feel, felt, found" approach. Practise verbalizing these responses *before* you use them with a customer.

THE POWER OF FIRST IMPRESSIONS

"You never get a second chance to make a first impression."

Nicholas Boothman, author of *How to Connect in Business*, contends that most people will make up to eleven different assumptions when they meet someone for the first time, and he states that these assumptions will be made within thirty to forty-five seconds. That means if the initial impression we portray is less than positive, we will have to work that much harder to gain credibility and earn the customer's trust. It also means we stand a lesser chance of closing the sale.

Years ago, my wife and I were looking for new living room furniture. The set we were considering was more than three thousand dollars, and the salesperson who was taking care of us was wearing clothing that was worn and outdated. He may have been well qualified to help us but because of the way he was attired my perception prevented me from seeing that. Here are a few hints and tips that will help you make a powerful first impression:

- Make sure your clothes fit properly and are clean and pressed.

- Pay close attention to the other person. Listen for his name and repeat it as you introduce yourself.

- Develop a great handshake.

- Create a thousand-watt smile and use it.

- Make excellent eye contact.

- Avoid overusing colognes or fragrances.

- Invest in the best pair of shoes you can afford, and make sure you shine them every time you wear them.

- Dry-clean your shirts to give them extra crispness.

- Pay attention to the eye color of the person you are meeting.

Make a great first impression, and improve your odds of connecting with your prospect and closing the sale.

SALES TIP

Review this list prior to your next sales meeting and make sure you make a powerful first impression.

THE POWER OF FLINCHING

"You want how much for this TV?!?"

One of the most effective negotiating tactics you can use to increase your sales is the flinch. A flinch is a visible and verbal reaction to an offer or price. The objective of the flinch is to make the other person feel uncomfortable for the request they made or the price they offered. Here is an example.

A customer asks you for a fifteen percent discount on a particular item. Your flinch would sound something like this: "You want me to give you a fifteen percent discount!?" If you are in a face-to-face situation, your body language and facial expressions should convey a message of surprise and concern.

I remember using this technique when I was buying carpet for my house. The owner of the store quoted a figure, and I responded, "Wow! That's a lot of money!" What was particularly interesting was how my wife responded to this. The owner of the store remained unfazed, but my wife started justifying the price of the carpet to me, not realizing I was using a negotiating technique.

There are two key things to remember when using the flinch.

1. Make sure that your facial expression and tone of voice indicate surprise. A flinch is not effective if you simply raise your eyebrows when the other person states their request.

2. Remain silent immediately afterward. In many cases, the other person will automatically bump up their offer or reduce the concession they want you to make.

The biggest challenge to using this technique is to step out of your comfort zone and allow yourself to act somewhat theatrically. I remember watching a sitcom many years ago called *Sanford & Son*. The widowed father would often pretend he was having a heart attack when his son made unreasonable requests.

SALES TIP

Practise using this strategy so that you become comfortable with it. When a customer asks you for a major discount or concession, respond with this tactic, then wait for their reaction.

THE POWER OF FREE OFFERS

"Ensure that the free offer does not cheapen the product or service."
Cy Charney, *The Instant Sales Pro*

Almost everyone likes to get something for nothing. In business, the key is to offer something of value, with no strings attached, to entice people to make future purchases. The best Internet marketers use this philosophy. They frequently offer a free book, consulting service, or product. Once people have discovered the value of the product or service, they are more willing to make a buying decision. Here are a few examples to consider:

- Many people offer free seminars or tele-seminars in their area of expertise. A tele-seminar is a short, forty-five to ninety-minute training session conducted on the telephone. Financial planners offer free seminars on estate or tax planning, investment strategies, and more general topics. The free seminars help create leads and generate business for other services.

- A speaker I know conducts a half-day workshop periodically and invites people on his mailing list to attend at no charge. He converts many of these prospects into new business.

- A real estate agent places an ad in the local newspaper and offers people tips and strategies that will help them sell their homes. In return, he captures their name and phone number and contacts them to see if he can represent them.

- Web designers can offer a free consultation or free web site analysis.

Other suggestions include:

- Giving someone a sample of your product to test. Wineries offer free tastings so they can sell more wine. Lots of food distributors set up sample tables in grocery stores; free samples lead to an increase in sales. Some authors allow people to read one or two chapters of their book online. In fact, one marketing guru began giving away electronic versions of his book in PDF format, and sales of the actual book soared afterward.

- Offering a free trial period. Many companies offer a thirty-day trial period to test their product. A car dealership I know will give a new car to a prospective customer for an entire weekend to help the customer make a buying decision.

Not every person who requests, or takes advantage of, your free product or service will turn into a client, but a free product can be a low-cost way to demonstrate the value of what you sell. Remember to offer something of value to the prospect, and make sure that there are no strings attached to the offer.

SALES TIP

Make a list of some of the products or services you could offer to a potential client. Ask a few friends if the value of your offer would entice them to contact you. Determine the cost of the offer and decide if you are willing to make the investment of giving it away.

THE POWER OF FOCUS

"You must remain focused on your journey to greatness."
Les Brown

The most successful athletes have the ability to focus so intently they block out the noise and distractions of the people in the stands. Sales professionals can benefit from this concept by developing the ability to concentrate on a specific task or outcome.

For example, if you want to increase your sales, focus on the activities that will help you accomplish this. In many situations, salespeople will avoid these activities because they are not the most enjoyable aspects of the job. However, by developing the discipline to focus on completing these activities, you will move closer to achieving your goals.

So, how can you develop this focus? According to the book *The Power of Focus*, written by Jack Canfield, Mark Victor Hansen, and Les Hewitt, it starts with eliminating bad habits and replacing them with healthy habits. Here are a few suggestions to get you started:

- Start setting goals (see Secret #40—The Power of Goals, for details on goal setting). In my opinion, goals are the best way to get focused, because once you set a target, your brain goes to work at achieving that objective.

- Seek out mentors to provide guidance. Mentors can help keep you on track and can offer direction when you are faced with challenges. Plus, they will challenge you and hold you accountable, which helps give you focus.

- Eat properly. Some foods improve your mental sharpness (fruits, vegetables, and fibers) while others (fats, oils, alcohol) decrease it. Increase your intake of high-quality foods and beverages on a daily basis, and your mental sharpness will automatically improve. Even drinking more water increases your mental acuity.

- Take regular breaks. Very few people can work at full capacity for extended periods of time. Take short breaks to recharge. Get up and stretch. Move around. Drink a glass of cold water. Eat a piece of fruit.

- When you are working on a project that requires concentration, turn off your telephone, your cell phone, and your BlackBerry, shut down your e-mail, and close your instant messaging system. This will help eliminate distractions.

Here is a completely different perspective on focus: Watch a basketball game. When a player receives a foul he is allowed to take one or two free throws. While the player lines up his shot, everyone in the stands yells, waves their arms, and tries to distract the player. However, most professional basketball players can block out these noises and distractions and focus on making the basket.

SALES TIP

Make a list of three or four activities that will help you achieve your goals, targets, and objectives. Select one item from your list and work on it until it is accomplished. This can help you develop your concentration.

THE POWER OF FOLLOW-UP

*"If you don't follow up, you risk losing
the sale to a competitor who will."*
Kelley Robertson

It never ceases to amaze me how few salespeople make the time to follow up after they have made initial contact with a prospect or customer. In the last few months, I can think of at least eight different situations in my own life (business and personal) when a salesperson did not bother taking this initiative. These included a landscaper who designed plans for our property, two different people who spoke to me about creating a promotional piece of literature for my business, a sales rep for a pool company, and a salesman who worked in a men's fashion store who was asked to send information. In each of these situations I was very interested in the product or service offered by the vendor.

This got me wondering...why don't people follow up? Here are several reasons.

They don't want to appear pushy. It may be true that following up too frequently will come across as being pushy. However, very few salespeople ever come close to crossing this line. In fact, one of the few times I left a salesperson who was pushy, it was more because of his tone than the fact he actually followed up. As a sales professional, I believe it is our responsibility to keep following up with our prospects until we know for certain if they want to do business with us. However, I also strongly believe that we can cross that line by making too many calls in a short period of time.

So where's the happy balance? It depends on your business. A weekly call is more than enough to keep in touch providing you make sure your call is short and to the point. Don't waste your prospect's time by droning on and on. Also, provide some additional value during your follow-up call whenever possible. This may give your prospect a reason to choose you instead of a competitor.

They forget. It's easy to forget, considering how busy we are. We may have every intention of calling our prospect but we get caught up in our business. Unexpected problems crop up, we find ourselves spending more time in meetings and stuck in traffic, and because we didn't schedule the follow-up it doesn't get done. This is a common dilemma but one that can be avoided by considering the follow-up as a scheduled appointment.

They make false assumptions. I once submitted a proposal to a company and told them I would follow up on a certain day and time. Unfortunately, I was extremely sick that particular day and it was several days before I recuperated. I then wrestled with whether or not I should call my prospective client. I was concerned he would question why I didn't call as scheduled. In the end, a simple apology was enough to rectify the situation and move the sales process forward.

When someone doesn't immediately return our phone call or e-mail message, we usually assume the worst—even if this assumption is not verified. I have learned from experience that a lack of response can often be attributed to the fact that the other person is just too busy to respond or does not have an answer for you.

They think the customer or prospect will contact them. I think this is one of the most common myths salespeople fall prey to. They think that if they do a good job the customer will automatically call them back—they don't need to follow up. Unfortunately, they cannot rely on this if they want to achieve their sales goals. People get busy, they forget or procrastinate, and the more time slips by, the less important your product or service may be to that prospective customer. I recall a situation when I expressed interest in buying a particular product from a store and told the sales associate I wanted to wait a little while. A few months later he called to inform me that the item had dropped in price and suggested that it would be an ideal time to buy. His follow-up reminded me of my interest in the product and motivated me to buy.

They have never been taught. Many salespeople have never received formal sales training and have not learned why they should follow up and how to make the follow-up happen. This is relatively easy to remedy. Start by asking or telling your prospect that you will follow up on a specific day or time. Tell him how you will follow up (telephone, e-mail, face-to-face) and record this in your day planner or time-management system so you don't forget.

They are afraid of rejection. Too many people who sell for a living would rather let a potential lead fall through the cracks than face the rejection that might occur. Instead of receiving a direct rejection, they decide it is easier to *not* follow through. However, this approach will not help you maximize your sales. Many people will end up doing business with the person who consistently follows up a proposal or request for information.

When did you last follow up with a customer to ensure she was satisfied with your product or service? If you are like most salespeople you probably have not followed up as consistently as you should. Unfortunately, most salespeople do not check in with their customers after the sale has been made.

The most common reason is that they fear customers will have a problem or concern. So, rather than dealing with this concern head-on, they choose not to call the customers. Yet they are missing a golden opportunity. If the customers are satisfied (and they should be, right?) the call will confirm to both customers and salesperson the value of the product and/or service. If the customers *do* have a concern or problem, then the salesperson is given the opportunity to correct the situation. Properly resolving a complaint will increase your sales and improve your brand in your customers' minds. There are several ways to follow up:

- By e-mail. Certainly e-mail is efficient, but it doesn't always deliver the proper tone and manner for effective follow-up. Plus, most executives already have too many e-mails awaiting a response.

- By card or letter. This style of follow-up is one of the least-used methods, yet it is very effective. I recommend sending a handwritten card within a few days of the purchase. Thank the customer for the purchase and remind her to contact you if she has any questions or requires any assistance.

- By telephone. This is the most effective approach, particularly if you send a thank-you card beforehand. If you receive voice mail leave a short message: "Hi Pat, it's Rick calling. I'm following up to make sure you are seeing results from the new software system we recently implemented. If you are not experiencing positive increases in productivity yet, please call me so we can discuss how to improve your results."

Here's the bottom line. You can easily differentiate yourself from your competition by making the effort to follow up with your prospects and customers. Don't take it for granted that they will call you. Be proactive and contact them.

SALES TIP

When someone expresses interest in your product or service but is not prepared to make a buying decision immediately, make a note in your time management system and contact the person later to see if he or she is ready to move forward.

THE POWER OF GOALS

"Give me a stock clerk with a goal and I'll give you a man who will make history. Give me a man with no goals and I'll give you a stock clerk."
J.C. Penney

One of the greatest motivators is to have worthwhile and meaningful goals to strive toward. Goals give you focus, clarity, and direction. Powerful goals will motivate and excite you. Goals can help you enjoy a fulfilling and rewarding life. Goals will cause you to grow. They will help you learn. Most important, they help ordinary people achieve extraordinary things. Here is the SMART method of setting goals:

S—Specific

M—Motivational

A—Achievable, yet challenging

R—Relevant

T—Time framed

Specific—Each of your goals must be as specific as possible. For example, setting a goal to increase your sales is a worthy target. However, the phrase "I want to increase my sales" is not clear enough. Rephrase this to, "I want to sell $10,000 this month," or, "I want to increases my sales by ten percent compared to last month." The more clear, concise, and specific your goal, the more focused it will be.

Motivational—As noted previously, your goals must motivate you. If you typically sell $60,000 in an average month, a goal of selling $61,000 this month will not be powerful enough to excite you to achieve it. However, if you set a target of selling $70,000 and becoming the top salesperson in the company, you will become motivated to achieve your goal. I know salespeople who are solely motivated to be the top performer each month. They do not set a specific dollar figure. Instead, they say, "I will have the highest sales in the company/division/department this month." They constantly monitor the sales figures of their co-workers and push themselves to stay ahead.

Achievable, yet challenging—Goals that are too easy to achieve will not keep you motivated. If they are too difficult to reach, you will become discouraged and lose your desire to work toward them. I believe that goals should have a seventy- to eighty-percent opportunity of success. Challenging targets will push you out of your comfort zone and cause you to learn and grow. Over the years I have discovered that we are capable of accomplishing much more than we think. I have set goals that were extremely challenging and achieved them because I believed in my ability to attain those targets. An associate of mine encourages people to set wildly ambitious goals rather than cautiously optimistic targets. This approach causes people to think far beyond their current situation and dream big dreams.

Relevant—Goals must be deeply personal. They must be relevant to your specific situation and your life. Avoid setting goals based on the opinion of other people. Determine what is important to you.

Time framed—Every goal must have a deadline—otherwise it is only a dream. Deadlines create a sense of urgency and help move you forward. I usually work on several projects at any given time. When I do not have specific deadlines, I tend to postpone working on them. However, setting targeted completion dates gives me the focus and sense of urgency needed to accomplish them.

Here are a few examples of SMART goals:

"To reach $15,000 in sales by the end of July."

"To sell 250 units of SKU number 18749 during November."

"To contact twenty new prospects this week."

"To acquire three new accounts worth at least $20,000 each by March 21."

Write your goals on paper. This step is one of the most powerful components of goal-setting. Writing your goals on paper helps drive them into your subconscious and acts as a catalyst to help you achieve your targets.

Review your goals twice a day—when you first wake up in the morning and immediately before you go to sleep at night. This will help you achieve them faster than you dreamed possible. This constant reinforcement drives your goals deep into your subconscious and helps you attract the people and events necessary to make the goals become a reality. The most successful sales professionals know how to harness the power of goals to achieve their targets. For more information on goal setting, visit www.RobertsonTrainingGroup.com and click on the "sales tools" link.

SALES TIP

Use the processes identified in this chapter and start setting sales goals for yourself. Begin with modest targets and gradually expand them as you begin achieving them.

THE POWER OF GUARANTEES

"And will you succeed? Yes indeed, yes indeed!
Ninety-eight and three-quarters percent guaranteed!"
Dr. Seuss

Many people are hesitant to buy from someone they are not familiar with, particularly if it is a first-time purchase and it involves a substantial amount of money. A guarantee reduces the risk and can eliminate buyer hesitations. Although many companies offer some form of guarantee, very few actually state it up front. I learned the value of offering a guarantee up-front shortly after I began my private practice.

I was discussing training workshops with two different companies, and both posed the question, "What happens if I'm not satisfied with the program?" I immediately told them that I would take whatever action was necessary to correct the situation and that if I failed to deliver the results we agreed upon, I would issue a refund. I closed both sales.

This experience prompted me to include a no-risk guarantee clause in all subsequent proposals. I have also applied the concept to my public workshops, books, and all the products I sell on my web site. What has been particularly interesting is how many people express their concern about the risk associated with this gesture. I'm frequently told how many people will take advantage of me and abuse this offer. Here is my perspective.

Yes, some people may take advantage of this guarantee. However, the increase in my sales will offset the number of people who request their money back. Besides, if I can't deliver the results I have promised I don't deserve to get paid. If someone truly feels that my products will not help him achieve better results, he should not have to pay.

The vast majority of people are honest, which means that you will seldom be required to make good on your offer. In my case, I have sold tens of thousands of dollars of products and have only been asked for a refund a few times.

The bottom line is that a guarantee can, and will, help you close more sales. Reduce the risk of doing business with you, and more people will buy your product or service.

SALES TIP

What type of guarantee can you offer that will reduce your customer's risk?

THE POWER OF HELPING OTHERS

"You can get anything you want in life if you just help enough other people get what they want."
Zig Ziglar

Salespeople who focus first on helping their customers and prospects typically fare better than salespeople who concentrate on closing the sale. I was reminded of this concept at the end of a training workshop to help improve coaching and leadership skills. One of the participants thanked me for the time I had invested with the group. He went on to ask how they, the participants, could repay me (the workshop was sponsored by their company). My reply was simple. They could concentrate on applying the concepts from the program and they could buy the books I had available. Afterward, there was a lineup of people waiting to purchase the books.

In addition to helping your potential prospects and clients, identify how you can contribute to your community. Donating your time, knowledge, and expertise is an excellent way to help others. Several times a year, I give pro bono presentations to different nonprofit organizations as a way of giving back. I can't speak to every group who asks me or donate books to every association, but I do set aside a certain number of days and amount of product each year. Decide what you can do to help other people and take action to make it happen.

You can also help other people by referring business to them. I often get calls from people who are looking for some type of training that I do not provide. I have no hesitation in referring them to someone else because I know this gesture will be rewarded. Plus, my goal is to help people achieve their business goals, and it makes sense to point them in the right direction.

SALES TIP

Determine what you can do to help other people achieve their goals. The more you focus on helping them, the more inclined they will be to help you.

THE POWER OF HONESTY

"If you tell the truth, you don't have to remember anything."
Mark Twain

Years ago my wife and I were in the process of buying a new washer and dryer. During the conversation, the salesperson mentioned that he owned the same set we were considering. However, he would not make eye contact as he expressed this statement. My instincts kicked in and I immediately felt that he was lying to me, which caused me to distrust everything he said from that point forward.

Unfortunately, the sales profession is fraught with dishonesty. That means many prospects and potential buyers are reluctant to believe the claims they hear. Think of situations you have been in when a salesperson has made a promise to you and failed to follow through. If you're like most people, this caused you to become less trustful of anyone who sells for a living.

Honesty in sales means:

- not selling a product or service to someone who does not need it

- being straightforward about delivery schedules, back orders, and so on

- not embellishing or exaggerating the capabilities of your product or service

- turning down a job that does not fall into your area of expertise

- refusing a kickback, bribe, or incentive
- acknowledging the people on your team who contribute to your success
- telling people about the shortcomings of your product/service when they ask
- refusing to do business with a person who acts in an unethical manner
- telling your clients about problems, concerns, and delays before they ask
- not misguiding people in order to close a sale
- avoiding the use of high-pressure sales tactics
- not lying to your customer, for any reason!

SALES TIP

Be honest when dealing with every customer, prospect, and co-worker. Never give people a reason to doubt you.

THE POWER OF HOT BUTTONS

"Look for the hot button, the reason the customer will buy, and press it."
Brian Tracy

Hot buttons are individual and personal motivators. Every person has specific motivators, and it is up to you to determine your customers' hot buttons in each sales situation. You do this by asking thoughtful questions and carefully listening to the answers.

Brian Tracy, professional speaker, trainer, and author, advises salespeople to question skillfully and listen carefully to every customer, because your customer will tell you everything you need to know in order to sell effectively. Here is an example:

Let's say you are a landscaper and you are talking to a couple about landscaping their yard. They run a home-based business and want to ensure that the first impression their clients receive is positive. The husband also says his main concern is that the yard needs to be low-maintenance because neither he nor his wife has the time or desire to take care of the garden. When you present your proposal, you should offer a weekly maintenance package, stressing how worry-free this will make the homeowners' lives. Reinforce the fact that the garden will look great at all times and will impress their clients. Tell them how easy it will make their lives because they will not have to spend their valuable time in the garden. Instead, they will be able to focus on tasks and activities that are more appealing to them.

You can use the same concept to sell business to business. Every buyer, purchaser, or decision-maker has certain hot buttons related to each individual sale. One of the ways to uncover these hot buttons is to ask: "What are some of the most important issues for you regarding this purchase?"

SALES TIP

Invest the time asking quality questions. Learn what is important to each customer and prospect. Find out what motivating factors are behind the buying decision, and position your product or service in a manner that addresses those factors.

THE POWER OF INFORMATION

"Information is power."

There is no question in my mind that this is the most important aspect of professional selling. I can look back on every sales interaction and tell you when I tried to shortcut the information-gathering process because in virtually every situation, I lost the sale. However, when I invested the time to learn about my customer's situation, goals, and objectives, as well as his needs and wants, I usually closed the sale.

Gathering information is a critical component of selling. After all, if you don't know much about your prospect's situation, how can you recommend the right solution? Gathering information means asking questions. High-quality questions. Questions that require your prospect to think. Most of the salespeople I encounter know they should ask questions but fail to do so during a sales interview.

I'm always surprised in my workshops when someone tells me that prospects will not allow them to ask questions. My experience has taught me that people will answer almost any question providing it is asked in a manner that will encourage people to respond. Most people want to talk about themselves and will answer the questions they are asked. It is usually the salesperson's bias that prevents him or her from actually asking the question.

Invest the time preparing a list of key questions to ask your prospects and clients. You may not ask all your questions but at least you will be prepared. You should refer to this list of questions every time you interact with a new prospect or are talking to an existing customer about a new product or service.

I also recommend that you ask mostly open-ended questions. This type of question will more fully engage your customers in the sales process and will help you learn more about them.

If you're dealing with executives, ask questions that focus on their goals and objectives. Avoid asking questions that concentrate on the details of the business, because in many cases, that executive will not know the answer—after all, she pays someone else for that!

SALES TIP

Create a list of high-quality questions that will assist you in helping your prospect make an educated buying decision. Practise asking these questions so you become comfortable with them.

THE POWER OF KEEPING IN TOUCH

"Differentiate yourself from your competitors
by keeping your name in your customer's mind at all times."
Kelley Robertson

A customer is a one-time buyer, while a client is a regular purchaser of your products and services. Most salespeople do not keep in touch with a customer after a sale has been made, but remaining in contact is an effective way to turn a customer into a client. This does not mean that you call a customer or client and waste time with idle chitchat. Instead, look for ways to contribute to the overall success of the customer's or client's business. Some strategies:

- Send a magazine article that will be of interest or value to your customer.

- Clip a newspaper story or press release that relates to your customer's business and send it to them.

- Mail a card when you hear news about a client's organization. This could include expansion plans, promotions, new product launches, and so on.

- Call to offer new information or tips that will help your client's business.

- Invite him to attend a sporting event or to play a round of golf.

- Take her to breakfast, lunch, or coffee.

- A speaker I know sends his customers postcards from the cities and countries he visits.

- Many companies send newsletters or magazines to their clients and customers.

- The real estate agent who sold us our house sends us a refrigerator calendar every year.

Each of these strategies is simple to execute and will help you stand apart from your competitors because very few salespeople take the time to keep in touch. I know people who set up a database to keep track of how keep in touch with their clients and prospects to ensure they do not send duplicate information.

SALES TIP

Create a system that will help you stay in touch with your customers and clients. What can you do to keep your name in their minds? You do not have to spend a lot of money on this. In fact, most of the ideas listed above are very low cost.

THE POWER OF
KISS

*"Making the simple complicated is commonplace; making the
complicated simple, awesomely simple, that's creativity."*
Charles Mingus

KISS stands for Keep It Short and Sweet. Too
many salespeople spend most of the time talking,
usually about nothing that is important to their client, customer, or
prospect. They spend too much time talking about their product, their
company, and their clients. But most customers don't care about this.
Instead they want to know what's in it for them. Here's an example:

My wife and I were in the process of buying a new car. At one
of the dealerships we visited, the salesperson droned on and on
about little details of the car. We had no interest in these details,
or we were already familiar with them. She told us about the power doors locks, power windows, and common dashboard items. I
wanted to go for a test drive but she kept talking about irrelevant
information. By the time we took the car out I had already made
the decision I would not buy from her, regardless of how well the
car performed during the test drive. It would have been much
better for her to ask a few questions about what was important to
us and she could have focused on those particular features.

Keeping your presentation short and sweet is an especially important
concept if you sell items of a technical nature. Describing how a complex product works, or explaining how to operate it, is challenging for

most people. The best salespeople know how to explain something that is highly technical in terms that anyone can understand. This is accomplished by speaking in non-technical terms and avoiding industry jargon or terminology. Another time to keep your explanation short and sweet is when you respond to objections. The majority of salespeople spend too much time trying to justify their product or price when a brief explanation is sufficient. Less is more when dealing with objections. Keep your explanation as simple as possible by focusing on the key points you need to make. Instead of listing every possible solution in rapid-fire style, state one answer and check to see if that response makes sense to your customer. Here is an example.

Let's say your customer has said that he doesn't see why he should buy the product from you because one of your competitors is less expensive. You can respond by telling him one thing that differentiates you from your competition. In this case, you offer 24/7 telephone support. Check and see if he sees the value in this. If not, offer one more suggestion. Continue this process until he does agree to buy from you or until you have exhausted the solutions. In most cases, you will overcome the objection more quickly than if you stated all the reasons to buy from you.

SALES TIP

Record your next sales presentation, and when you return to the office or home, listen to the recording. Pay attention to how much extra or unnecessary information you discuss, and work at eliminating it.

THE POWER OF KNOWLEDGE

"Knowledge is of no value unless you put it into practice."
Anton Chekhov

Knowledge is a powerful weapon for anyone who sells. Here are some of the things you need to know:

1. An excellent knowledge of your products and services is essential if you want to be successful in sales. Learn the key features of each product and know how to explain the benefits of each feature. See Secret #11—The Power of Benefits for more information about selling benefits.

2. Know what your competitors sell and how your products and service compare. It surprises me how many salespeople do not invest time learning about their competitors. Every business has intense competition. It is critical that you find out as much as you can about competitors' business, products, service, warranties, post-sale support, service, and so on.

3. Know who the key decision-makers are in the organizations you call upon. Too many salespeople try to sell their product to the wrong person. If the person you are speaking to is not the sole decision-maker, then you need to get in touch with the person who

is involved in the sales process. You can approach this without offending your contact by asking something like, "Who else do you normally talk to when considering a decision of this nature?" If you can uncover this information, your next step is to arrange a meeting with that individual.

4. Know how best to present your products and services. This means being able to explain your offering in terms that every customer can understand. You must adapt your approach, use different analogies and examples, and focus on what is important to the customer you are presenting to at that particular time.

5. Know the most challenging problems your customers face. Invest the time to learn about industry trends, challenges in the industry, and your customer's competitors. This will help you determine the best way to present your product/service and demonstrate how it will solve your customer's problem. When you can solve a customer's problem, price becomes less of an issue, and you differentiate yourself from your competition.

6. Know how to rephrase a question when you don't get an answer that helps you. This approach helps people articulate their thoughts and makes it easier for you to learn more about their situation.

7. Know the best time to contact or call upon your customers. One way to quickly determine this is to ask, "What time of day works best for you to talk?" Some people prefer meeting in the morning (I'm one of those) before the day gets wound up, while others would rather meet later, when the day is coming to a close. Remember, it's not what works best for you; it's what is best for your customer.

The more knowledge you have about products, services, customers, and competitors, the better you will be able to position yourself.

SALES TIP

What do you need to know about your clients, prospects, company, competition, products, and services, in order to close more sales?

THE POWER OF LANGUAGE

"Change your language and you change your thoughts."
Karl Albrecht

The words we choose influence the people we speak to. Consider these phrases:

"Oh, we're out of stock."

"We can't get any until next month."

"That item is on back order."

"We can't arrange delivery until next week."

"All we have left is a demo model."

These statements demonstrate negativity and can influence a customer's decision. Our goal is to turn these negative statements into positive ones, such as:

"We're completely sold out!"

"They're selling so fast we can't keep them in stock!"

"We can have that for you by next month."

"I can have that delivered to you next Tuesday."

"We have a display unit available that works great."

You'll notice that rephrasing a sentence or using a few different words can change the entire message the customer will hear. When we emphasize the right words with the appropriate tone of voice, the result will be a positive message. Here are more:

Instead of saying ...	Replace it with ...
I can't do that.	Here's what I can do.
You should have...	In the future I would suggest...
I didn't do it/It wasn't my fault.	Let me help you resolve this.
I don't know.	Let me find out.
But... We can order that for you but it will take three weeks for it to be delivered.	Replace the word "but" with a period (.) and begin a new sentence. For example, We can order that for you. It will take three weeks for delivery.

These small, subtle changes make a difference in the message your customer will hear and in how your message is perceived.

SALES TIP

Pay attention to the words you use in your sales meetings and conversations. What message are you delivering to your customers?

THE POWER OF LISTENING

"We have two ears and one mouth so that we can listen twice as much as we speak."
Epictetus

Great salespeople are also great listeners. I have watched salespeople ask high-quality questions only to ignore the answer or response the customer gives them. If you are not going to listen to the other person, there is no point asking questions.

I remember a salesperson asking me a variety of questions only to launch into his standard presentation immediately afterward. This told me that he had not listened to the information I gave him during that sales interview.

Being patient and listening to your customer can present some great opportunities. I once listened to my wife on the telephone with someone who contacted us about using one of my articles in their publication. I have written and published dozens of articles and receive frequent requests for reprints. In this particular situation, my wife sensed that the person on the other end of the telephone had more to say after his initial opening and monologue, so she remained silent and simply listened to him. A few moments later he told her that his budget for an article of this nature was only $150. If I had been talking to this person, I probably wouldn't have discovered this because I would have been quick to offer the article at a lower price. I often notice that salespeople ask a question, then give their customer the answer, or continue to talk instead of waiting for a response. Once you ask a question, refrain from speaking, and allow your customer to talk. You will learn a great deal more about people when you actively listen to them. People will tell you anything you want to know, you just have to ask—then listen.

SALES TIP

During your next sales meeting, make the effort to listen more than you talk. Employ active listening techniques such as nodding your head, restating or summarizing what people tell you, and using prompters such as, "uh-huh" and "go on."

THE POWER OF MARKETING

"You cannot not market."
Peter Urs Bender

Many people mistakenly think that marketing and advertising should be lumped into the same basket. However, it is important to recognize that advertising is part of an overall marketing strategy.

How you market yourself will influence others' decisions to buy from you. Marketing is an extension of your image and part of your brand. It is how you represent yourself and your business to people in the marketplace.

This means that everything you do as a sales professional is some form of marketing. How quickly you respond to customer requests, how you deal with their concerns, and the way you answer the telephone, all contribute to your marketing message.

So, what is the best way to market yourself and your product? There is no one way that is most effective. The best approach is to use a variety of methods to promote your product and/or service. Here are a few ideas that can help:

- Write articles to establish yourself as an industry expert.

- Develop a postcard campaign to keep your name in your prospects' minds.

- Give short speeches at local Chamber of Commerce meetings, Rotary and Lions clubs, and industry associations.

- Ask for referrals.

- Create referral alliances.

- Send articles to prospects and customers.

- Place ads in trade magazines.

- Have lunch with one new contact every week/month.

- Run a contest in your area and tell the local newspaper about it.

- Fully utilize your business card by printing an overview of your services on the back.

- Offer a free "how to" report.

- Attend events where your ideal clients will be.

- Join networking groups.

- Piggyback on other events such as trade shows, conferences, and association meetings. Partnering with other people can give you great exposure at a fraction of the cost.

- Participate in Internet chat rooms, forums, and online discussions.

- Create a blog (web log) and update it regularly.

- Send well-written sales letters to prospects, customers, and clients.

- Publish a newsletter.

- Create and launch a great web site.

- Send out a broadcast fax with a special offer.

- Give a free presentation to help your target market improve their results.

- Invite your customers to a VIP day.

- Ask other people to mention your products/services on their web site or in their newsletters.

- Run seminars, workshops, or programs.

Ultimately, there is no limit to how you can market your business, and many of the strategies mentioned here will cost you very little.

SALES TIP

Use a variety of strategies, and implement one new approach every week or month to keep your marketing fresh and interesting.

THE POWER OF NEGOTIATING

"There's an art to deal-making and negotiating, and it's an art that few people possess."
Donald Trump

I'm always surprised how many salespeople quickly discount their product or service in order to get the sale instead of taking the time to negotiate an outcome that works for everyone—the customer, the salesperson, and the company for whom the salesperson works.

Negotiating does not mean offering an ultimatum—a "take it or leave it" approach. If a potential customer uses this tactic, I recommend turning down the deal—unless, of course, it makes good business sense to accept the offer. Here are some principles to keep in mind the next time you enter a negotiation:

- Don't say yes too quickly, even if you like the deal. Make the other person feel good by having to work for it.

- Avoid discussing price too early. The more quickly price comes up in the discussion, the more of a focal point it will become. When confronted with "How much do you charge?" I recommend that you defer the question until you have established the value of your goods or services. One of the ways you can do this is to say, "It's not fair for me to quote a price until I've learned more about your particular situation." Then ask a few questions that will help you position yourself more effectively.

- Information is absolutely essential. The general rule of thumb is that the person with the most information will fare better in the negotiating process. That means you need to ask plenty of questions to fully determine your prospect's situation. In addition to possessing a great knowledge of your products, services, and company, you also need to know who your competitors are and how they compare to your organization.

- Never hesitate to negotiate. Many people resist negotiating because they feel embarrassed. This hesitation and embarrassment can be overcome by taking the time to practise. Starting with small-value situations can help you develop your confidence, and gradually you will become more comfortable negotiating for larger dollar value purchases.

- Set high goals. People who aim higher usually end up doing better than people who set low targets for themselves. In most labor disputes, people ask for much more than they know they will get. The union will ask for the moon and stars while the company offers very little. Both sides know that these initial demands and concessions act as anchors. Later, when the dust settles, they usually meet somewhere in between.

- Be aware of deadlines. This is a particular challenge for salespeople who often face monthly quotas. If you are close to the end of the month and you need another sale to reach your target, the deadline will usually influence your behavior and often cause you to make concessions you might not normally agree to.

- Make your concessions slowly, and don't give away your profit margins too quickly. It's easy to forget that we are giving away money when we make concessions. Imagine how the conversation would change if there was a big stack of cash on the table, between you and your customer, and every time a person asked for a concession, he took that amount of cash out of the pile. I'm confident that your approach and attitude would change pretty quickly.

- A frequent mistake is to make too many assumptions. We often assume that our customer is not willing to pay our price, because we believe everyone is concerned only with getting the best price. A friend of mine once went to an electronics store to replace a stolen camera. The salesperson mentioned an extended warranty and offered a significant discount on it without being asked or without realizing that my friend was willing to pay full price for the additional coverage.

Negotiating does not have to be adversarial. In fact, when the right approach is used, negotiating can turn into a dialogue between you and your customer.

SALES TIP

Resist the temptation to offer a discount or reduce your price too quickly. Instead, invest more time at the front end of the sales process. Ask questions about your customer's situation, needs, and wants. Then focus on demonstrating the value of your product or service.

Visit www.RobertsonTrainingGroup.com for free articles and additional resource materials that will help you learn how to negotiate more effectively.

THE POWER OF NETWORKING

"The successful networkers I know, the ones receiving tons of referrals and feeling truly happy about themselves, continually put the other person's needs ahead of their own."
Bob Burg

Sales are frequently developed through the relationships we have created with people. Networking functions provide the opportunity to expand our contact list, particularly when we create and nurture quality relationships. It is not enough to visit a networking group, talk to dozens of people, and gather as many business cards possible. However, every networking function has tremendous potential for new business leads. Follow these five strategies to make networking profitable:

1. **Choose the right networking group or event.** The best results come from attending the appropriate networking events for your particular industry. Events should include trade shows, conferences, and associations dedicated to your type of business. Or, join a group or association where many of the members are potential clients. For example, an associate of mine helps businesses negotiate leases with landlords. Because many franchised organizations lease their properties, he became a member of a franchise association.

2. **Focus on quality contacts versus quantity.** Most people have experienced the person who, while talking to you, keeps his eyes roving around the room, seeking out his next victim. This individual

is more interested in handing out and collecting business cards than establishing a relationship. My approach is to make between two and five new contacts at each networking meeting I attend. Focus on the quality of the connection and people will become much more trusting of you.

3. **Make a positive first impression.** Develop a great handshake and approach people with a natural, genuine smile. To make great eye contact, notice the color of the other person's eyes as you introduce yourself. Listen carefully to people's names. If you don't hear them or understand exactly what they say, ask them to repeat it. Many people do not speak clearly or loudly enough, and others are very nervous at networking events. Make a powerful impression by asking them what they do *before* talking about yourself or your business. As Stephen Covey states, "Seek first to understand and then to be understood." Comment on their business, ask them to elaborate, or have them explain something in more detail. As they talk, make sure you listen intently to what they tell you. Once you have demonstrated interest in people, they will—in most cases—become more interested in you. When that occurs, follow Step 4.

4. **Be able to clearly state what you do.** Develop a ten-second introduction as well as a thirty-second presentation. The introduction explains what you do and for whom. For example: "I work with boutique retailers to help them increase their sales and profits." This introduction should encourage other people to ask for more information. When they do, you recite your thirty-second presentation. "Bob Smith of High Profile Clothing wanted a program that would help his sales managers increase their sales. After working with them for six months we achieved a 21.5 percent increase in sales. Plus, sales of their premium line of products have doubled in this time frame." As you can see, this presentation gives an example of your work and the typical results you have helped your clients achieve. Every introduction needs to be well rehearsed so you

can recite it at any time and under any circumstance. You must be genuine, authentic, and as I heard another sales trainer say, "bone-dry honest."

5. **Follow up after the event.** In my experience, most people drop the ball when they leave the event. Yet the follow-up is the most important aspect of networking. There are two specific strategies to follow:

First, immediately after the event—typically the next day—you should send a handwritten card to the people you met. Mention something from your conversation and express your interest to keep in contact. Always include a business card in your correspondence.

Next, contact those individuals again within a few weeks and arrange to meet for coffee or lunch. This will give you the opportunity to learn more about their business, the challenges they face, and how you could potentially help them. This is *not* a sales call—it is a relationship-building meeting.

The more people know about you and your business, and the more they trust you, the greater the likelihood they will either decide to work with you or send you a referral.

Networking can be a very effective way to increase your sales. But you must choose networking groups carefully and use the right approach.

SALES TIP

Determine the best events for you to attend. Set a goal of meeting two or three people and learning as much about their business as possible. Look for ways you can help them, and eventually they will help you.

THE POWER OF NEWSLETTERS

"Keep your name in your prospect's mind."
Kelley Robertson

A newsletter can be an extremely effective way to keep in touch with existing clientele and to generate additional sales. The most cost-effective way to distribute a newsletter is electronically. Although newsletters can be issued in paper format, this approach is much more expensive and time-consuming. Here are a few pointers to keep in mind as you create your newsletter:

Ensure that you offer practical or valuable information. I have subscribed to some newsletters only to find that they are nothing more than thinly disguised advertisements. It is okay to promote your products or services. Just make sure that your newsletter contains solid content. Otherwise, the number of people who unsubscribe will outnumber new subscribers.

Your newsletter should be issued on a regular basis. Whether it is a weekly or monthly newsletter, make sure that you send it out on the same day or date so people will start to anticipate its arrival. My goal is to offer a bit of motivation to kick-start my subscribers' week, so I issue my weekly tip every Monday morning before 9:00 A.M. On the rare occasion I am tardy in sending it, I usually receive several e-mails from my subscribers asking when it will be issued.

There is no standard length for an electronic newsletter. I receive some that are less than a hundred words and others that are several thousand words.

If your publication is too short, it will be difficult to share any meaningful information. If it is too long, people may not read it.

Make sure you include an "unsubscribe" feature or link, so your readers can opt out of your newsletter. I get very frustrated when people don't give me a way to stop receiving their literature.

Make sure you check your spelling and grammar before you send your e-mail out. Your professionalism is reflected in the quality of your newsletter, and in the number of typos and mistakes.

Consider the format. Html-style newsletters are more visually pleasing because they allow graphics and colors, but some spam filters block them. Plain text can be easier to read (although less pleasant to look at) and will often pass through spam filters. Your content will also determine whether you get through the spam blockers. Words such as free, offer, sale, sales, guarantee, and anything that can be perceived as pornographic will trigger spam filters and may prevent your newsletter from reaching its intended receivers.

Use an outbound e-mail service such as Aweber, Constant Contact, or Motion4.com. I know some people who use their regular e-mail system and use the b.c.c. feature. However, many ISPs (Internet Service Providers) limit the number of recipients you can send your e-mail to, which means sending your newsletter will take more time. Outbound e-mail servers allow you to send an individual e-mail to each of your subscribers with the click of a button.

Newsletters that offer useful information are consistently read. In many cases they are forwarded to other people or printed and posted for team members to read. I have many subscribers who use my weekly tip as the focus for the week. They post the tip for everyone to read and often conduct brief meetings to discuss how they can incorporate the topic into their business.

Anyone can use a newsletter to market and promote a business. Regardless of what you sell, you can offer practical advice or feedback to potential buyers.

SALES TIP

Start collecting names and e-mail addresses. Develop a short newsletter and start sending it out to your contact list.

THE POWER OF ONE

"One is the loneliest number."
Three Dog Night

One is a very tiny number. However, it can have a tremendous impact on your revenues. Imagine the difference in your results if you:

- made one more cold call every day
- arranged one more appointment each week
- suggested one additional item to every customer
- asked for the business one more time with each prospect
- invested one day per month in developing your skills
- read one book related to your industry every two weeks
- asked one more question during each sales call
- got to the office one hour early
- addressed one more objection before giving up
- sent one more e-mail to the prospect who has been sitting on the fence
- asked one more client for an endorsement or testimonial
- made one more call before heading home

- scheduled one more breakfast or lunch meeting with a potential client

- paused for one moment before responding to a prospect's question or request

- suggested one more idea to help a customer improve their business

- reread your sales letter one more time

- established one more goal to achieve

- added one more testimonial letter to your web site, brochure, or marketing materials.

One can be a very powerful number. One extra sale every day, week, or month, depending on your business, can make a significant impact on your sales by the end of the year.

SALES TIP

The next time you think about giving up on a high-potential prospect, consider that you might be just one phone call, e-mail, or letter away from making the sale.

THE POWER OF PAINTING MENTAL PICTURES

"Sell the sizzle, not the steak."
Elmer Wheeler, *Tested Sentences That Sell*

"And for dessert, we have this incredible Bombastic Brownie that will electrify your taste buds. We start with a fresh homemade brownie that's warmed up until it is piping hot. We add two scoops of rich French vanilla ice cream, then drizzle chocolate fudge over the top. Then we swirl fresh whipping cream over that and top it off with a bright-red maraschino cherry. It's only $4.95."

Are you drooling? Can't you visualize this luscious dessert in your mind? Compare that presentation with this one: "And for dessert, we have a brownie with ice cream. It's $4.95."

Experienced restaurant servers understand the importance of using descriptive words to enhance their dishes. You, too, can use this concept when talking about your products or services. Create images that correspond to your customers' psychological needs. Help them visualize the ways your product will enhance their lives, reduce stress, increase comfort, or make them more productive. Show them how simple your product is to use, or describe how their friends will respond to their having it. Draw them into your presentation; get them excited about what you are selling.

Compare a high-quality training seminar to a university lecture. In the lecture you listen passively; at the seminar you participate actively.

Which role do you enjoy the most?

The movie *Just the Ticket* dramatizes this concept. Andy Garcia plays a ticket hustler who desperately wants to date the Andie McDowell character. In one scene the Andie McDowell character agrees to have dinner with him if he can sell a home-theatre package to a blue-collar worker. Garcia's character presents the television and corresponding equipment to his customer with passion, emotion, and a variety of descriptive phrases. He captures the customer's attention and interest, and the customer decides to buy the system.

Mental pictures draw customers into your presentation and captivate them. Your images make your presentation more interesting, more pleasing to listen to, and easier to remember.

SALES TIP

Create a list of descriptive words and phrases that relate to your products and services. Incorporate these words and phrases into your sales presentations.

THE POWER OF PARTNERING

"When we seek to discover the best in others,
we somehow bring out the best in ourselves."
William Arthur Ward

"Get the sale at any cost."
"Make more calls."
"Tell them what they want to hear."

Sales professionals in most industries are under tremendous pressure to close sales. It is not uncommon for them to hear comments similar to the three above from their sales manager, supervisor, or boss. But the approach described in these comments does not create trust with a customer and does not encourage repeat business or a lasting relationship.

A more effective approach is to develop a partnering relationship with your clients. This means working with them to help them achieve their goals and objectives. Simple in theory, the strategy requires a completely different approach. Here's what I mean.

In the majority of sales meetings, the salesperson looks for ways to position his or her product or service so the customer will buy it. In a partnering approach, the salesperson puts his or her goals and objectives aside. In the partnering approach you focus one hundred percent of your attention on your customer. The approach requires a selfless mind-set because there are situations when the best solution is not your solution. In fact, you may have to tell your customer to contact a competitor. I have experienced this several times. People contacted me about delivering a particular service, and although I may have been able to help, I knew someone who could better meet the requirements. It was mentally difficult, but I made the decision to refer these people to the competition.

Partnering also means that you provide exceptional follow-up to ensure that your customers are completely satisfied with their purchases. This does not mean you make just the obligatory follow-up call. It means you explore their actual use of your product or service and help them maximize its full potential.

A client was experiencing less than favorable results after implementing a new program into his business. We scheduled a follow-up meeting with the management team, because as the vendor, I knew that the answers lay in the execution of the program. During the meeting we explored several ways to improve their results, and one of the solutions required me to provide some additional follow-up. Although I could have charged my client for this time, I knew that it made good business sense to absorb the cost of the extra follow-up because my primary objective was to help my client achieve the best results possible. Subsequent meetings indicated that this investment was worth it, as my client began discussing how we could take this initiative to the next level.

The challenge with the partnering relationship is that most salespeople want some form of instant gratification. Partnering does not always offer a direct or immediate payoff for the salesperson. However, from a business perspective, the partnering concept makes good sense.

It is also important to note that you don't necessarily have to give away additional service. Some sales trainers incorporate telephone coaching into their proposals. They charge for the phone call, but they position the charge as a way for the company to improve its results. They demonstrate how the additional investment will drive more dollars to the client's bottom line. Ultimately, your goal should be helping your customers and clients improve their business results. Here are a few points to consider.

1. **Focus on your client's goals and objectives instead of your personal agenda (closing the sale).** If necessary, recommend another supplier or vendor who offers the exact product or service your client needs.

2. **Follow up.** Contact your customers and talk to them after they have made a purchase. Ask them if they are getting the desired results. If they aren't, look for ways to help them maximize results. Offer additional support. Give extra resources. Help your clients get the best results possible.

3. **Incorporate a systemized process into your sales pitch or proposals.** People will pay for extras providing they see the value that is brought to their organization.

4. **Send information to your customers on a regular basis without being asked.** I like to regularly send my clients and prospects articles that are relevant to their businesses. This demonstrates that I am looking out for their interests, rather than my own.

When you help your customers achieve their goals and objectives, you become more than a supplier or vendor. You become a preferred partner. The partner relationship will prevent your competition from overtaking you in the marketplace.

Create a checklist of the additional services you can offer to your clients to help them achieve their goals. Helping your customers reach their objectives will help you increase your profits.

One word of caution: this is a process, not a quick fix. This strategy does take time to generate a return. However, it is well worth the investment.

SALES TIP

Create a list of what you can do to become more of a partner with each of your customers.

THE POWER OF PASSION

"Do what you love and the money will follow."
Marsha Sinetar

Passion is a critical component of successful selling. I have witnessed many new salespeople outperform their seasoned co-workers even though they lack knowledge about their product or service. This is usually due to the level of passion and excitement they possess.

Unfortunately, most people lack passion in what they do. They spend eight or ten hours a day at work, doing something that does not really interest them. My wife once spoke to someone who possessed an excellent ability to fix computers. In fact, he was our computer technician for a few years. However, his true interest was making jewelry. When my wife suggested that he pursue his passion, she was told that he needed a job with a regular income and that fixing computer problems allowed him to pay the bills. Then he would be able to enjoy his passion as a hobby.

I learned many years ago the importance of doing what you are passionate about. The more passionate you are about your career, the greater the chance you will succeed. The reason for this is simple—when you love what you do, you put more effort into your work. When you are passionate about the products or services you sell, your enthusiasm will shine brightly in every conversation.

If you aren't genuinely excited about selling your particular product or service, give serious consideration to making a change. You are not doing yourself, your company, or your customers any favors by continuing to represent something you can't get excited about.

The challenge for many people is to find this passion. One way to start is to begin exploring an area of personal interest. As soon as you start taking action, you begin to program yourself at a subconscious level to watch for anything related to this interest. You will notice things that you previously disregarded. You will tune into conversations pertaining to the topic.

Another approach is to consider what you enjoy doing. Here is an example. A participant in one of my workshops played in a band, but he really enjoyed producing music, and before long sought out a career in this field. The advantage of doing what you love is that you will likely invest the time and effort required to make your career a success.

Here are a couple of questions to ask yourself that can help you determine what you really enjoy. The first is, "If you knew without a doubt that you could not fail, what would you do?" The second is, "If you had to devote your life to doing one thing, what would it be?" Please consider these questions from a business perspective, not a social one. In other words, don't answer with responses like, "I'd watch television all day," or, "I'd hang out with friends."

SALES TIP

If you do not have passion for what you sell, consider a change. Ultimately, you are not doing yourself or your company any favors by selling a product or service you do not believe in.

THE POWER OF PATIENCE

"Our patience will achieve more than our force."
Edmund Burke

Successful sales professionals have developed the ability to be patient. They don't hurry through the process because they recognize that rushing will cause them to make costly mistakes. Patience can be difficult, particularly when you have many sales calls to make or several customers to see.

I once contacted a company about buying a mailing list. A salesperson returned my call within twenty-four hours, we had a lengthy discussion about what I needed in a mailing list, and he e-mailed me some information to review. In the next ten days he called me four times. The first two calls were made on the same day. And each time he called, he pressed me to make a decision. The fourth message he left had tones of impatience and frustration, and he gave the indication that he wanted to get this sale and move on to his next customer. At that particular time I was extremely busy and I had not had a chance to look through the information he e-mailed to me. His impatience annoyed me, and I decided not to use his services.

I understand the importance of following up after an initial meeting or sales call. However, there is a fine line between a professional sales approach and pestering your customer to make a buying decision.

We have to remember that businesspeople are extremely busy. Unless a customer has a pressing need or high sense of urgency for a product or service, she will seldom make a decision quickly. I once spoke to a couple of executives in one of the companies with whom I work. During our conversation one executive said, "Just when I think I can't get any busier, I do." The other executive agreed and added, "I get a dozen voice-mail messages from salespeople every day but I ignore them because I already have too many projects to complete. Even if their product has some merit and value, I just don't have time to focus on anything new or to even meet with the salesperson."

Too many salespeople fail to look at things from their prospect's perspective. Just because you think your solution is important does not mean it will be a priority to your prospect. Priorities shift every day, especially the higher up in an organization you go.

SALES TIP

Look at things from your customer's perspective. Recognize that people in business are busy. Develop a follow-up strategy to keep in touch with your contacts.

THE POWER OF PAUSING

"The right word may be effective, but no word was ever as effective as a rightly timed pause."
Mark Twain

The pause is an effective interviewing technique and it can be used in the sales process too. Here are some situations in which pausing can be very effective.

After you ask a question. I have watched many salespeople ask their customer a question then continue talking. This prevents the other person from responding and will limit the amount of information you learn. Avoid giving people an answer to your question. Remain silent for a moment or two and give them the opportunity to answer.

When you want a particular point of your sales presentation to sink in. Every sales presentation has key points that are more important than others. You can help a customer digest these key points by pausing after presenting one. This gives your customer time to process what you have said. In many situations, this pause will also encourage her to ask a question, which gives you the chance to elaborate on your product or service.

Before you respond to a question. A friend of mine always pauses before he answers someone's question. This allows him to process what the other person has said and demonstrates that he is thinking about his response, which shows a high degree of professionalism. Unfortunately, most salespeople simply wait for their turn to speak instead of listening intently to what their customer says.

When you are not exactly sure what to say. Pausing can give you a few extra moments to think of an appropriate comment. A business consultant I know was unsure how to respond to a new prospect's question. While he struggled to think of an answer, the prospect answered his own question, and the consultant closed the deal.

Don't be afraid of the temporary silence. Most people appreciate a few moments of silence during the sales process. See Secret #84—The Power of Silence for more information on this topic.

SALES TIP

Practise pausing during every sales meeting and telephone call. Notice how other people respond and watch to see what additional information they give you as a result of your pause.

THE POWER OF PERSISTENCE

*"Nothing in this world can take the place of persistence...
Persistence and determination alone are omnipotent."*
Calvin Coolidge

Several years ago I accompanied my youngest daughter on a school ski trip. She had never skied, and after a few lessons, stood atop the practice hill. During the next few hours she fell many times as she practised her newly acquired skill. However, by the end of the day she was able to ski down the entire hill without incident. It took her dozens of attempts. She fell numerous times. But each time she got up, brushed away the snow, and continued her efforts. She refused to give up until she accomplished her goal.

Persistence is a critical attribute for anyone who sells for a living or who owns a business. In their book *Attitude, Your Internal Compass*, Denis Waitley and Boyd Matheson tell the story of a military leader who marched into battle against the opposition six times, and each time his army was driven back. Feeling somewhat defeated, the soldiers eventually took refuge in a cave. As the leader pondered how he could rally his troops to mount another attack, he noticed a spider trying to build its web. To get the web started, the spider needed to jump across an opening. The leader watched in fascination as the spider attempted to complete the jump. The spider failed to land in the proper location in the first several jumps but, undaunted, kept trying. On the seventh attempt it landed in its desired location and was finally able to place the first strand, then create the web. The leader took this as a sign that he must be resilient and engage the opposing army at least one more time. His resilience inspired his troops, and they conquered the enemy on the seventh attempt—and saved their kingdom.

In 2003 I ran my second full marathon (26.2 miles). I had trained for several months and felt ready for the race. At the halfway point I felt great; I was running at a comfortable pace and was actually overtaking many other runners, which prompted me to increase my pace. Three miles later I began running out of steam, but I still had more than ten miles to run. The desire to quit was almost overwhelming. However, I kept telling myself that quitting was not an option. Failure was not part of my game plan for that run. I slowed down and began taking walking breaks. Eventually, the finish line came into sight, and I crossed it with a huge smile on my face. I did not achieve my desired time but I did finish. Persistence won out.

So, how do these stories apply to sales?

I remember reading a study that found eighty percent of salespeople stop trying to contact a potential prospect after approximately three to five attempts. The same study showed that it took an average of at least seven to nine contacts to close a sale with a new customer. That means that the majority of people give up too soon. They don't connect with a prospect after a few attempts, so they stop calling.

A close friend of mine was once embroiled in a business lawsuit. After a lengthy battle, he finally triumphed with a unique solution. When I asked how he thought of the solution, he told me it was the last thing he could think of. His refusal to give up helped him come up with the answer that would solve his problem.

Selling requires a tremendous amount of persistence. Obstacles loom in front of us on a regular basis. But it is what we do when faced with these barriers that will determine our level of success. A person will face the most challenging obstacle just before he achieves his final goal, and the most successful salespeople in any industry have learned to face the obstacles that get in their way. They look for new ways to connect with prospects. They are tenacious. They refuse to give up, because they know that persistence will help them achieve their goals.

SALES TIP

The next time you encounter a roadblock, make the decision to look for a new or different approach. Keep trying until you have exhausted every alternative. This tenacity will often result in a sale.

THE POWER OF PERSONAL DEVELOPMENT

"Strength and growth come only through continuous effort and struggle."
Napoleon Hill, *Think and Grow Rich*

The majority of successful sales profession-als invest in their personal development. Of course, as a trainer, I have a certain bias on this topic. When I worked in the corporate world, I was constantly on the lookout for programs and workshops that would help me improve my results. I once at-tended a sales-related conference, and in one of the breakout sessions, which focused on negotiating, I sat next to a seasoned salesperson who had more than seventeen years of negotiating complex sales. When I asked him why he was attending this particular session he said he felt he could always learn something new, or at the very least, refresh some of the skills he had developed. I realized that part of his success was a result of continually looking for ways to improve his results.

This lesson stayed with me, and now, as a business owner, I continue to invest in my personal development. In fact, I now invest more on an annual basis than I did when my employer was footing the bill, because this investment has consistently helped me achieve better results.

Personal development can mean attending seminars or workshops. It can consist of reading books, magazines, or newsletters (electronic or pa-per), listening to CDs, watching videos, or participating in tele-seminars.

Networking and meeting other professionals in your field can also help. Some of the best ideas I have had were a result of conversations with friends, associates, or other professionals in my field or industry. A good friend of mine always attends our industry conference because he always learns something new from others in the field.

I recommend that at the beginning of each fiscal year, you identify the resources that will help you become more successful in your chosen field. Here are a few sample topics to get you started:

- improving your prospecting skills
- managing your accounts
- selling to senior executives
- improving your sales presentations
- overcoming objections
- marketing yourself and your business
- writing effective proposals
- using networks to increase your sales
- cold calling
- dealing with voice mail
- managing the complex sale
- creating long-term client relationships
- connecting with people
- maintaining your motivation
- negotiating more effectively
- improving your communication skills
- improving your listening skills
- improving your closing skills
- dealing with difficult customers

This is just a partial list of topics. I'm sure you can come up with more topics that are relevant to your specific business, industry, or situation.

You can find books, DVDs, CDs, workshops, and web sites that provide information on any of these topics. The key is to apply the information you gain. Changing your approach is not easy. It requires focus as well as patience. You must be willing to experiment with new ideas, to try different techniques and strategies, to step out of your comfort zone. With a little bit of discipline and courage you can dramatically improve your results.

SALES TIP

Make a commitment to continually improve your skills and expand your knowledge. Tap into the resources that are available to you. If you incorporate one new concept into your approach every month you will soon rise above your co-workers and competitors.

THE POWER OF PLANNING

"It pays to plan ahead. It wasn't raining when Noah built the ark."

I am surprised how few sales professionals, independent consultants, and small-business owners take the time to plan a strategy for their business. Most people spend more time writing out a grocery list or planning a vacation than they do planning the direction or goals of their business. Many people have a vague or general idea of what they want to accomplish, but very few identify the specific action steps they need to take to achieve their goals. I'm not suggesting you create a twenty-five or thirty-page business plan, like a good friend of mine writes every year, but I do recommend that you begin outlining your goals and how you plan to achieve them.

It is one thing to set a target for yourself; it is quite another to plan how you will achieve it. When I establish my annual goals (which get more challenging every year), I ask myself, "How will I accomplish these goals?" The question forces me to plan tactics, strategies, and actions to undertake so I will achieve my targets. For example, if my business relies primarily on referrals, I identify what I can do to increase the number of referrals I receive.

In her book *Get Clients Now!*, C.J. Hayden suggests using a monthly tracking sheet. This means setting specific monthly goals, planning what action you will take to generate new business, and tracking your progress.

She suggests that you engage in a minimum of ten different marketing activities each week. These can include networking, prospecting, cold calling, sending mailers, and speaking. A speaker I know invests most of his Mondays planning and strategizing his week, determining exactly what activities he will execute in the upcoming few days. Then he spends the rest of the week executing his plan.

How should you plan your business? It all depends on what you want to accomplish and what is important to you. Only you can determine what is important. And this will change depending on what stage of life you are in. What is important to you now may be completely irrelevant six months from now. Here are five key areas to plan:

Revenue. If your business is like most businesses, you likely have more than one product or service. Therefore, breaking down your sales into specific categories makes sense. The breakdown will allow you to track your progress in each area and see where you can improve year over year. You can also determine which products or services don't generate very good sales.

Profit. Obviously, determining your gross sales is important. More important, though, is the amount of money you have left over at the end of the day. In other words, what profit are you going to generate? A professional speaker I know plans his business by deciding what profit he wants to earn each year. He then creates his plan backward to determine how he will achieve his goal. Remember, you can generate incredible sales but still go out of business if your expenses are too high.

Expenses. Controlling expenses is a critical aspect of running a profitable and successful business regardless of the size. All large organizations budget expenses, but most independent business owners wing it and pay the bills as they come in. If you want to increase your revenues, you need to know how much it will cost you to generate your targeted sales. I remember talking to another trainer a few years ago who had learned this lesson. She began analyzing all her expenses and found several areas she could trim. She freed up cash, which she used to market her business. The result was more revenue with no additional out-of-pocket expenses.

Vacation or Personal Time. How much free time do you want for yourself in the next year? I have learned that it is very easy to get sucked into the vortex of running a business and forget to take a vacation or personal time to recharge my batteries. Block off some personal days in your calendar early in the year. This signifies a commitment and allows you to plan your business around these personal days. A friend of mine spends most of his summer scuba diving, so he plans the rest of the year accordingly. He works extremely hard, which frees up almost three months for him to partake in his favorite pastime. Incidentally, he has now turned this passion into a revenue center.

Personal Development. I have found that the people who invest in themselves consistently outperform those who don't. Identify the skills that will help you become more successful. Determine what books, programs, courses, or people can help you learn these skills, and take action.

SALES TIP

Make the time in your hectic life to create a plan for next the week, month, and year. Review your plan regularly and make the necessary changes as you progress. Planning does take time. However, it is time well invested.

THE POWER OF POSITIONING

"The best positioning is put in the context of solving a problem for a specific buyer."
Steve Johnson, *Pragmatic Marketing*

How you position your product or service often influences your prospects' desire to do business with you. Most salespeople have a tendency to pitch their offering too soon, then recite a list of generic features and benefits. I remember looking at a new car, and the salesperson spent the first five minutes of her presentation telling me about the power windows and door locks—features that I was already very familiar with.

If you truly want to separate yourself from your competition, you must position yourself differently. That is why it is so important to uncover the specific needs of each individual prospect, customer, and client.

Gathering the necessary information from your customer helps you position your product or service in a manner that is most appropriate to that customer.

Let's say you sell new cars and you have learned that your customer is most interested in the way the car handles on the highway. Rather than talk about horsepower, torque, or how fast the car accelerates, focus on showing the customer how it handles, feels, and responds at highway speeds.

When positioning your product or service, speak in terms that your customer can relate to. Use language she can understand. Demonstrate how your product or service meets her specific need or concern. Ultimately, if you want customers to buy your goods or services, you need to be able to show them how they will benefit.

SALES TIP

Decide how you can position your products and services differently than your competition. What makes your product or service better than your competitors? What do you do that your competitor doesn't? Why should someone buy from you versus someone else?

THE POWER OF POWERPOINT

"What you say is more important than how you say it."
David Ogilvy

I believe PowerPoint has become the most overused and misused piece of software on the planet.
However, it does serve a purpose and it can definitely improve the overall
appeal of your sales presentation, providing you use it properly.

One of the biggest mistakes salespeople make is to rely on PowerPoint
as their presentation. I have been on the receiving end of too many sales
presentations where the salesperson booted up a laptop and walked
through a PowerPoint slide show—in most cases, reading the presentation from the slides.

PowerPoint software should be used to reinforce key points rather
than to deliver all the information. And there are several key points to
keep in mind when designing a presentation:

- Limit your text to six words per line and six lines per page. You do
  not need to include paragraphs of text. Font size should be at least
  24, if not more.

- Use graphics whenever possible. Many people think at an abstract
  level, and graphics tend to capture attention, particularly when
  they relate to the topic at hand.

- Avoid complicated charts or graphs.

- Do not use the software's animation or sound features. While they may appear fun on your computer, they usually do not add value to your presentation. Business people are not impressed with fancy animations—they want to know how your product or service will help them solve a problem.

- Limit your use of transitions. PowerPoint is loaded with dozens of different transitions for slides and text, but most of them detract from, rather than add to, a presentation.

- Take a course. Most people are self-taught when it comes to this software, primarily because it seems so easy to use. However, I have learned that you can save a tremendous amount of time by taking a course and learning how to properly create a presentation. A good instructor will teach you some of the most common presentation mistakes and how to save time when you create a presentation.

Remember, it's the information that you want people to remember, not the cute slide show.

SALES TIP

Review the ideas listed in this chapter the next time you need to create a Power-Point presentation.

THE POWER OF PRACTICE

"It's not necessarily the amount of time you spend at practice that counts; it's what you put into the practice."
Eric Lindros

Professional athletes constantly practise to develop their skills. After a day of tournament play, golfer Tiger Woods will head to the driving range and hit two or three buckets of balls. Hockey and football teams repeat drills and practise certain plays time and again so they can properly execute these plays when it counts the most—in the game. Baseball players take batting practice and pitchers practise different pitching techniques.

Sales professionals should also practise several different things:

1. **Call scripts.** Before picking up the telephone and making that call, you should practise your script a few times to warm up. Run through it so your voice sounds natural and relaxed. Change the emphasis on certain words and phrases to hear the difference. Call your voice mail and recite the script as a message. Afterward, listen to how your script sounds and make the necessary changes.

2. **Sales presentations.** The most effective sales presentations are not delivered on the fly—they are rehearsed, timed, and in some cases even choreographed. I'm not suggesting that you script out everything in your presentation. However, you should have a clear idea of what you're going to say and how you plan to say it. If you are using

any audio or video tools to enhance your presentation, practise using them *before* your presentation—and make sure you have a plan B in case something goes wrong. I remember a salesperson trying to gain access to his web site to show me a feature of his product. Unfortunately, access was denied, and he was crestfallen because he didn't know how to demonstrate his service without the web site.

3. **Responses to objections.** Every sales professional hears objections in the course of the job. You can become more effective in overcoming these objections if you anticipate them and prepare your responses. If you typically hear three or four objections on a regular basis, you should develop several standard responses that will help you overcome these objections. Practise reciting these rebuttals several times until your answers flow naturally and smoothly. This will develop your confidence and competence in this aspect of the sale.

4. **Responses to commonly asked questions.** Most salespeople hear the same questions frequently. Be prepared for these questions. Have stories, analogies, examples, case studies, and testimonials ready to go and know when to use each. Remember to keep your answers as clear, concise, and brief as possible

5. **Asking for the sale or for some form of commitment.** Many salespeople are uncomfortable asking for a commitment from their customers. I suggest that you create a list of different closing-style questions—ones that you would feel comfortable asking. Invest a few minutes asking these questions aloud. This will help your brain and mouth work together and will develop your confidence in this area.

6. **Asking for referrals.** Many people are uncomfortable asking for referrals. They don't want to sound needy or desperate, or they are concerned that they will come across as pushy. Again, practise. Ask for referrals in different ways until you find an approach that works well.

SALES TIP

Make the time and effort to practise your skills. While it may seem tedious at first, the results you achieve will more than pay off for you.

THE POWER OF PREPARATION

"Success always comes when preparation meets opportunity."
Henry Hartman

Proper preparation is critical if you want to be successful in sales. If you are meeting a prospective customer with the intent of discussing how your product or service can benefit him, you must do some preparation. You can:

- Browse your prospect's web site and learn as much as possible about the company *before* your meeting.

- Read their annual report.

- Talk to employees within the company to learn about their corporate culture.

- Identify possible market opportunities for your prospect.

Most of the salespeople I encounter invest very little time preparing for their meeting or sales call. In many cases, they end up wasting my time because they attempt to sell me a product or service that has no relevance to my business.

When you prepare for a sales presentation, you should anticipate the questions your prospect may ask you. Determine what examples, case studies, or success stories you will share. Identify what objections your prospect might state and decide how you will respond.

Before you head out for your appointment, double-check to make sure you have everything you need. I have made the mistake of forgetting a key piece of literature or a testimonial from a client. This mistake reduces your professionalism and limits your opportunities to deliver your best during the sales call.

Part of the preparation process includes knowing where all of your information is located in your briefcase or portfolio. You reduce your professionalism by having to fumble through your materials to find a specific piece of information. Be prepared. Look prepared. Act prepared.

SALES TIP

The more important the sales call is to you, the more time you should invest preparing for it. You get exactly one opportunity to make a dynamic first impression—make sure you are ready for your meeting.

THE POWER OF
PRESENTATIONS

*"It takes one hour of preparation for
each minute of presentation time."*
Wayne Burgraff

As a sales professional you will be required to present your product or service. In some cases, your presentation will be to an audience of one. In other situations, you may be required to present to a group of buyers or company representatives. Regardless, your ability to effectively articulate your thoughts and ideas and talk about your company, products, and service will influence your audience's decision to buy from you. Here are a few guidelines to keep in mind:

- Identify the key points you want to make and the relevant information for each point. Your primary goal is to show how your product or service will help your prospect in his business.

- Picture the person(s) who will attend your presentation. Focus on their radio station WII-FM (What's In It For Me?) and format the presentation to address their key objectives. I once worked with a person who seldom had an idea rejected because he always made sure that his presentation spoke to the concerns of the individual(s) to whom he was presenting. The presentation is not about you—it is about focusing on what is important to the other person.

- Keep the number of key points limited to three or four at most. Each of these topics can have subtopics, but your main presentation should consist of as few points as possible.

- Add spice to your presentation by incorporating a variety of tools and resources, such as video, multimedia, endorsement letters, case studies, audio testimonials, PowerPoint, and so on. A friend of mine is also a sales trainer and when he meets with new prospects, he often stands up and uses the boardroom whiteboard or flip chart to explain some of his information.

- If you plan to use PowerPoint in your presentation, keep it brief. Avoid making the mistake of using PowerPoint to deliver your entire presentation. Instead, use this resource to reinforce the key points of your presentation. Also, whenever possible, use graphics, and limit the amount of text on your slides—the general rule of thumb is six lines of six words each per slide.

- Avoid talking at great length without involving your prospect, customer, or client. A ten-minute monologue about your company is one of the fastest ways to turn off a potential customer. Once again, focus your presentation on how you can help your prospect solve a problem—increasing sales, reducing expenses, improving productivity, decreasing employee turnover, eliminating costly mistakes or procedures. Avoid discussing all the features of your product, particularly when you are presenting to high-level executives.

- Practice is essential. Do *not* attempt to give an important presentation that requires the use of a variety of media without first running through it.

Too many salespeople fail to think of the impact of their presentation. The quality of your presentations reflects on you and your business. Make sure your presentations are the best they can be.

SALES TIP

Determine what you can do to improve the effectiveness of your sales presentations.

THE POWER OF PRODUCT KNOWLEDGE

"The dumbest people I know are those who know it all."
Malcolm Forbes

There are two aspects of this topic that are important.

1. You need to know as much as possible about your product or service.

2. You need to be able to present this knowledge in a manner that makes sense to your customer.

Let's deal with number one first. A sales professional knows how her product works, knows each of the features, and can describe the benefits to her customer as well as the possible shortcomings and limitations. This may not be possible when you sell complex products or solutions. That means it is important to develop a good relationship with product designers, engineers, or technicians who service your product. Use these individuals to help you when a customer asks in-depth questions about your product.

One word of caution—before you head into a sales meeting with two engineers by your side, brief them on the importance of speaking in lay terms. Many technicians get mired in details and can talk for hours about their products. They often speak in technical terms, which means that many customers may not understand how the product will benefit them.

The second point is being able to discuss your product or service in terms that make sense to your customer. Many salespeople feel compelled to tell their prospect everything about their product and/or service. But few people care about everything the product offers. In most cases, there are just a few features that stand out for any particular customer. It is important to accurately assess what each prospective customer wants or needs.

Asking the right questions helps you learn exactly what your customer wants. You can then adapt your presentation to address the customer's specific needs rather than deliver a generic sales pitch.

You also need to use language that is familiar to your customer. Too many salespeople use technical jargon or acronyms that do not mean anything to their customer. This happened to me when I developed my web site. Both my webmaster and web host provider used terminology that went way over my head.

When I first began creating training materials I was instructed to write them in terms that an eighth-grader could understand. This did not mean that I had to talk down to my participants—it meant that I had to keep the learning points simple. The easier your make it for people to understand how your product can benefit them, the greater the chance they will do business with you. Some of my clients sell complicated digital products. The sales literature they are given is written by product specialists and it usually does not make sense to the average person. These salespeople must be able to explain this complex information in everyday language.

My wife is a software instructor. When she teaches people she uses everyday terminology that anyone can understand. For example, when she is teaching people how to set up files, she says that the My Documents folder acts like a filing cabinet. Each folder contains a category of information, and within that folder the clients will store files. She gives examples of the typical folders people create so her clients can relate to what she is saying. When people leave her session, they have the knowledge and confidence to use their computers effectively and efficiently.

SALES TIP

If you notice a blank look in your prospect's eyes you have probably overexplained your product. Simplify by using analogies that relate to your customer's specific situation. A truly effective salesperson makes it easy for customers to understand the product or service.

THE POWER OF PROMPTNESS

"Punctuality is the soul of business."
Thomas C. Haliburton

Time is a precious commodity for most business-people today, especially executives. That means we need to arrive on time for our appointments. We need to call when we say we will call. And we need to get to the point as quickly as possible.

A participant in a workshop once told me he was surprised I had arrived early for my presentation. Arriving early allowed me time to talk to attendees, assess the group I was speaking to, lay out my materials, and mentally prepare for my presentation. In another situation, a client commented that I called at exactly the time I said I would. In both situations, I was simply doing what I had committed to.

Most people have a tendency to run late for meetings, appointments, and sales calls. I experience this all the time in my workshops. People blame the traffic, weather, and unforeseen circumstances. But the bottom line is that they didn't plan to arrive on time. Certainly there are times when traffic or weather can cause delays. However, in most situations, we can avoid being late if we take the time to plan beforehand. I strongly believe that, if I am not at least fifteen minutes early for an appointment and sixty minutes for a presentation, I am actually late.

Promptness also means responding quickly to client requests. In today's competitive world, you cannot afford the luxury of waiting to respond. A marketing consultant I know tells people he will return telephone messages in four hours or less, which means his clients know they can count on him to return their calls quickly, which means they will not have to wait for information.

Promptness also means that you get to the point of your sales call as quickly as possible. Business executives are busier than ever before, and we have to respect that. Avoid wasting time on small talk unless your prospect initiates it. An effective strategy is to ask your prospect how much time she has allotted for the meeting *before* you show up at her office. If she has blocked sixty minutes in her schedule and you know can get through your presentation in less than forty-five minutes, you can spend a few minutes on social chatter and small talk. Plus, if you finish early you will gain her respect. However, if she told you she has only scheduled thirty minutes, then you will need to get to the point very quickly. A sales professional knows how to shorten a presentation and still cover the key points.

SALES TIP

Think of aspects in your business where promptness could help you increase your sales or competitive advantage. Then devise a plan to increase your promptness in these areas. Plan to arrive at appointments and presentations early—you never know what might hold you up. If you do arrive early, use those extra minutes to plan for the next call, return a couple of phone messages, check your appearance, or review your notes in preparation for the meeting. You'll be relaxed, prepared, and on time.

THE POWER OF
PROPOSALS

"Requests for proposals (RFPs) are cold.
Warm them up with a personal touch."
Len Serafino, *Sales Talk*

Depending on the type of product or service you sell you may need to create a proposal from time to time. The majority of proposals that are submitted tend to be overly complicated and difficult to understand. Here are a few tips to improve the readability and comprehensibility of the proposals you create.

Start with an executive overview. This section highlights your customer's key objectives and identifies—in point form—how your product or service will help your customer achieve those objectives. The executive overview should be clearly stated on the first page of your proposal. You can start with a section titled "Key Objectives" followed by a bullet-point summary of how your products or services will meet those objectives.

Next, include the details of your solution. Explain how the solution will be implemented. Identify who will be responsible for each item and the process that will be required. This section should be written in lay terms so anyone reading the proposal can understand exactly what will happen and who will be involved.

Use headlines for each key point. In my proposals, I use headlines for the workshop format, implementation procedures, timing, ROI (return on investment), and my guarantee. Whenever possible, use bullet points, because they are easier to read and understand.

Make sure you include how your customer will benefit from each point. You need to state, in concise terms, the payoff to your customer. Here is an example: one hotel chain offers its preferred guests sixty-second check-in, which saves them time by allowing them to bypass any lineup. As a frequent traveler, I dislike spending time in lines, so this benefit appeals to me because I know I can get to my room quickly after spending the day in transit. Although explaining the benefits sounds like a simple concept, most salespeople fail to state the benefits of their solution to their customer.

Summarize your proposal. Some people will flip to the last couple of pages of your proposal to look at the costs. If they haven't read through the entire document, you may lose the opportunity to create value. Include a summary of services you and your company will provide at the end of your proposal. The summary gives you an additional opportunity to demonstrate the value of buying from you. The summary should be written in point form and should recap everything in your proposal.

When you price your products or services, I think you should break prices down by line item. This allows your customers to see exactly what they are paying for and how much each item costs. If you plan to include additional value-added services as part of the contract, it helps to associate a specific dollar figure to each item. For example, I offer my clients unlimited e-mail support for one year after a training workshop. This means every participant can e-mail me with a question or problem, and I will respond. The value of this service varies, but on average, the value is $149 per person, so I state this in my proposal. My clients know they will receive that extra value at no additional charge. If I include my book or one of my CDs as part of the program, I state the value of the publications. This increases the overall value of my offer and can help differentiate me from my competitors.

Last, keep your proposal as brief as possible. One of the key things I have learned is that executives are extremely busy. They don't have time to review a forty-page document. The more concise your proposal, which will include relevant points and benefits, the greater the likelihood that your prospective client will read it.

SALES TIP

Evaluate the proposals you send to prospects. Does your proposal recap the essential points of your prospects' needs? Does it demonstrate the benefits of your products or services? Is it easy to navigate?

THE POWER OF PROSPECTING

*"Sales are contingent upon the attitude of the salesman—
not the attitude of the prospect."*
W. Clement Stone

Most salespeople do not invest enough time in prospecting, particularly when they are busy. But prospecting now determines your future sales.

Too many salespeople wait until business is slow before they start prospecting. Unfortunately, this approach will cause peaks and valleys in your results. One month will be great and the next month will be slow. I remember a conversation with an accountant who specialized in working with small-business owners. He told me that everyone who owns a business should set aside at least one day a week for marketing and prospecting. He recommended that I block this day in my schedule and use it to generate new leads. His advice still rings in my ears to this day.

Everyone prospects differently, and there is no one way that works the best. Cold calling works well for some people. For others, prospecting means attending networking functions a few times a month. Some people find that sending letters, e-mails, or postcards works, while others think that following up on referrals is the best approach. Ultimately, you need to find what works best for you. Here are a few prospecting strategies for you to consider.

- **Contact prospects by telephone using a carefully selected list.** Many companies specialize in selling lists. Once you identify your target market or clients you can ask a list-management company to generate or create a list of prospective customers. Then you pick up the phone and dial for dollars. Make sure you have a well-developed script. Don't wing it.

- **Use the Internet.** I receive numerous calls from people trying to sell me a product because they have come across my name on the Internet. One word of caution with this approach—make sure you do your research before you contact prospects. Don't waste their time trying to sell them a product or service that has little or no relevance to their business.

- **Network.** This can be a great prospecting tool if you attend the right networking events. I spent almost two years going to a multitude of networking events because I thought it was the right thing to do. I soon learned that it is critical to attend the events your prospective customers attend. It is also important that you learn something about the people you connect with. I have attended some events, given my business card to someone, and then received unsolicited mail from that person. Not every individual at a networking event is in your target market.

- **Use e-mail lists.** E-mail can be a very cost-effective way to reach a large number of people. You can send a blanket e-mail to thousands of people for just pennies, but it is seldom a qualified list of people. I once thought (naively) that anyone and everyone who signed up for my weekly e-mail newsletter was a potential customer. Even though these individuals found value in my newsletter, only a few have turned into clients for my workshops. However, many of them have bought CDs, books, or e-books, or participated in tele-seminars.

- **Use trade directories.** Depending on the type of product you sell, this can be a good prospecting tool. If you use directories, make sure the materials you send prospects are relevant to their situation. I have received countless calls and pieces of mail from association members who have no idea what I do or who my target market is.

- **Use the telephone book.** This may seem like an unlikely source of business, but I have used it to create a list of businesses to contact.

- **Read the newspapers.** Newspapers can be a great prospecting tool. You can review the classified ads, highlight stories of companies who have been mentioned, and make a list of organizations that advertise in the paper.

- **Read trade publications.** I know a business owner who contacts people who have been featured on the cover of a trade magazine and asks if they are interested in his products and services. He doesn't always get the business, but his approach is unique.

There is no one right way to prospect. However, by using a variety of approaches you increase your visibility.

SALES TIP

Devote a specific amount of time to prospecting each and every month. Determine the best approach for your business and make sure you keep prospecting for new business even when you are busy. This will help you avoid peaks and valleys in your business.

THE POWER OF PUNCTUALITY

"If you are not at least fifteen minutes early, you're late."

Imagine the consequences for a band if they arrived at a venue just a few minutes before they were scheduled to play. They wouldn't have time to ensure their equipment was properly set up or to conduct a quality sound check. And their performance would likely be mediocre at best.

Yet at a conference I attended, one of the speakers entered the ballroom just as he was being introduced. He raced to set up his slide show, and his subsequent presentation was harried and rushed as he stumbled through his information. This confirmed the importance of arriving early for sales calls, presentations, and client meetings.

Traffic in most urban centers is always congested. You need to arrive with time to spare so you can de-stress after the traffic and delays you may have encountered. The last thing you want during an important meeting with a prospect or client is to be distracted by annoyances that occurred during your trip to their office. Arriving early is essential if you are traveling to an unfamiliar destination.

A friend said he had an important sales call with a new client in a city that was a one-hour flight away. His appointment was scheduled for 5:00 P.M so he booked a late-morning flight. When he arrived at the airport he discovered that his flight had been delayed by two hours. No problem, he was sure he still had plenty of time. By the time he arrived at his destination he still had more than an hour to drive to his client's office, which was less than ten miles away. He picked up his rented vehicle and headed to his appointment, only to encounter construction delays. His anticipated fifteen-minute highway drive ended up taking triple that time, and although he was on time for his appointment, he felt a certain amount of stress by the time he arrived.

I once read that you should allow twice the amount of time required when traveling to an appointment. While this extra time may seem excessive, it can certainly give you the necessary buffer to take care of any physical setup requirements, and it allows you time to review your notes and mentally prepare for your presentation.

Ultimately, it's better to be early for an appointment than late, especially if you are meeting with executives.

SALES TIP

Plan to arrive at least fifteen minutes early for your next meeting or sales call. Invest the time you have available prior to your appointment to review the purpose of your meeting and the key points you need to remember.

THE POWER OF QUESTIONS

*"One who asks a question is a fool for five minutes;
one who does not ask a question remains a fool forever."*

I firmly believe that most salespeople do not ask enough questions. Based on conversations in hundreds of sales-training workshops, I have determined that there are several reasons people do not ask questions.

- They have never been taught.
- They think that selling means talking about their product or service.
- They are concerned that their customer might say something they can't respond to.
- They feel it takes too much time.
- They think people will find questions intrusive.
- They don't know what questions to ask.

Each of these reasons is valid. I have consistently found in my business that the more questions I ask early in the sales process, the more sales I close. I quickly discover who is a qualified prospect versus someone who is fishing for information (a suspect) and I also find out if I am capable of helping that person. In many cases, I can't help the people who contact me because I don't offer the appropriate type of program. However, I can refer these individuals to other people in my network.

Virtually every sales book contains a chapter stressing the importance of asking open-ended questions. Many salespeople have been taught to ask open questions, but my experience as a trainer and consumer has taught me that most people ask closed questions.

Open questions begin with what, where, why, who, when, and how. They require your customer or prospect to think about his reply, which means he cannot shrug off the question with a yes or no. He is expected to give you information. There are a few challenges associated with this concept.

First, many salespeople do not ask open questions because they cannot anticipate the answer. With a closed question, you expect either a yes or a no response, which means you can prepare your rebuttal even before the customer has answered. With an open question, though, a customer can say anything. This means a salesperson is not able to plan a response ahead of time.

Many salespeople also think open questions take too long. Some customers talk at great length when given the opportunity, and asking them an open question gives them this opening. I have found that, in most cases, the information people share helps me better understand their situation and needs. With that information I can create a proposal that addresses the key issues they face. This strategy results in a higher closing ratio.

Open questions should focus on your prospect's needs, wants, goals, objectives, corporate culture and values, market-share opportunities, existing challenges, and future plans.

When you develop your open questions, keep in mind who will be responding. When you speak to executives, you must keep your questions focused at a high level. Avoid asking about day-to-day issues, because many executives are not involved with this aspect of the business. However, it is unlikely that buyers within a company will be thinking about the strategic direction of the company when they speak with a salesperson.

SALES TIP

Make a list of open-ended questions you can ask to learn more about your prospects and customers. Practise reciting these questions until you become comfortable with them. Then use them when you speak to new prospects and existing customers. Here are some examples to get you started.

- What challenges are you currently facing in the marketplace?
- Who else do you normally talk to when considering purchases of this nature?
- What features are most important to you?
- When were you thinking of moving forward with this project?
- What concerns do you have about this purchase?
- Who are the key decision-makers in your company?
- How does a decision like this generally get made?
- Who else should we get involved?

THE POWER OF RECHARGING YOUR BATTERIES

"Laughter is an instant vacation."
Milton Berle

Selling for a living can be a tiring proposition, especially if you travel extensively. A well-rested sales professional is alert. She is able to respond appropriately to objections and customer concerns. Her presentations have more focus, and her energy level is higher. She knows that her results are a direct reflection of how rested she is.

In a perfect world we would all get eight hours of sleep every night. However, we all know that such a world does not exist. That means we must take other action to ensure we get enough rest to recharge our batteries. A few simple strategies that can help include:

- Take frequent breaks throughout the day. This is more difficult than it sounds. A hectic schedule means that it is not uncommon to skip lunch or grab a quick bite from a fast-food drive-through. I remind myself to drink lots of water during the day. This forces me to take short bathroom breaks, giving me the chance to get up, stretch, and move around.

- Allow time between appointments. When you have back-to-back meetings scheduled with different clients or prospects, it is easy to catch yourself racing between these meetings, which causes stress and decreases your performance level and productivity.

- Experts say that a twenty-minute nap in the afternoon restores your energy. I'm not suggesting you curl up under your desk, but if you can arrange it, I do think a short nap can revitalize and rejuvenate you. However, be careful not to fall into a deep sleep; otherwise you will find it difficult to get going again.

- Take vacations. Very few people can work at 100 percent capacity for months on end. Vacations are a great way to rest and recharge. You don't have to travel to an exotic country or stay at an expensive resort, either. Sometimes, spending a few days catching up on your reading is all it takes.

- Get physical. Many busy salespeople and executives get involved in some form of physical activity. Mountain biking, golf, sky-diving, racing, playing organized sports, and running are all ways you can recharge your batteries. It doesn't matter what you do, the key is to participate in some form of physical activity to relieve your body of the stress it accumulates.

- Get a massage. Most people underrate the effectiveness of a massage. This can be a great way to relax and recharge yourself at the same time. Many companies have a health-care program that covers an occasional massage from time to time. Take advantage of this offering. A really good massage can loosen the knots, kinks, and stress that build up in your body.

SALES TIP

Determine the best way you can recharge your batteries, and take action to make it happen.

THE POWER OF RECOVERING FROM DEFEAT

"It is inevitable that some defeat will enter even the most victorious life. The human spirit is never finished when it is defeated...it is finished when it surrenders."
Ben Stein

The most successful people in business have learned how to recover from defeat. They have faced many obstacles and have developed the skill and ability to bounce back quickly. Yet I have seen many people who have stewed about a particular failure or a lost sale for many months. From my perspective, this just cripples them from achieving their true potential.

We all face obstacles in our career and business. It's how we respond to them that makes a difference. The most difficult challenge I ever faced was losing my job many years ago. For the better part of a year I accepted the role of the victim and avoided taking responsibility for what had happened to me. My self-confidence slipped, my performance dropped, and my effectiveness declined noticeably. However, when I accepted responsibility for my job loss I soon found that my attitude changed. I changed my focus. I began to work harder. And I focused on providing more value to my new employer so the same thing would not happen again. It was the best learning experience in my entire life. Since then, I accept accountability for every sale I have lost. It's not always easy, but assuming this responsibility has helped me become better at what I do.

I have learned that a missed sales opportunity is usually a direct result of something I have done or failed to do. In most cases, I have neglected to ask the right questions or have proposed a solution that does not accurately address my prospect's needs.

It also helps to have some form of support group. I don't mean getting together with a group of people to bitch, moan, and whine about life. I believe in having people you can talk to who will give you honest and open feedback. Individuals who will offer an objective perspective. People who aren't afraid of telling you exactly how they see it.

Mentors can fall into this category because they have usually faced similar experiences themselves and can relate to the situation. Because of this, they have the unique ability to offer practical advice and help coach you through the situation.

SALES TIP

Determine how you will deal with setbacks and defeats. Is a support network your best alternative? Or, will you get on the telephone and contact several new prospects?

You can also ask your prospect why they didn't accept your proposal or why they chose to use another supplier or vendor. This information will help you become more successful in future sales calls. Regardless of the approach you use, it is critical that you take some form of action immediately.

THE POWER OF REFERRALS

"No matter how artful or talented you are, you must follow a specific methodology to be successful in expecting and getting quality referrals."

Scott Kramnick, *Expecting Referrals*

The referral is the one of most effective ways to generate new business. A solid referral can open doors, warm the initial contact, and make your prospect more accessible. Unfortunately, most people do not capitalize on this concept. Many sales professionals are uncomfortable asking friends, clients, and prospects for referrals because they do not want to appear needy, greedy, or aggressive. But there is more to it than just asking people you know for the name of someone they know. You need to implement a system. Here are some ideas to get you started.

First, you need to clearly identify your ideal customer so you can tell people the type of person to look for. The more specific you are, the easier it is for someone to make a referral. For example, rather than saying, "If you know someone who could benefit from my services, have them call me," say, "I help first-time home buyers find their ideal home. If you know someone who is looking to buy their first home, I'd appreciate it if you could connect us."

Second, you must ask. Too many salespeople assume that they will receive referrals simply by delivering good service. Unfortunately, the majority of people do not think of referring a friend or co-worker. That is why you must remind people to give you referrals.

Third, you must ask consistently. Create a system to ensure that you ask *every* customer, client, and prospect for a referral. The best times to ask for a referral are:

- Immediately after you have made contact with a prospect and he has turned you down.

- Immediately after a customer has agreed to do business with you.

- After the sale has been concluded and the service and/or product has been delivered.

It is also important to *give* referrals. Too many people expect others to refer business without reciprocating—this is particularly noticeable at networking events. One of the fastest ways to increase the number of referrals you receive is to actively look for opportunities to direct someone to another business (noncompeting of course!).

I also think it is critical that you recognize people who refer business to you. At the very least you should send a thank-you card. Depending on your type of business, a referral fee may be in order. Many people give the referrer a commission or discount on future purchases.

SALES TIP

Make the effort to give referrals to noncompeting businesses. Define your ideal customer and create a system to remind yourself to consistently ask for referrals.

THE POWER OF RELATIONSHIPS

"Business is not just doing deals; business is having great products, doing great engineering, and providing tremendous service to customers. Finally, business is a cobweb of human relationships."
H. Ross Perot

Relationships are a key way to develop new sales opportunities. In fact, many books have been written about the importance of relationship selling. Few business decisions are made without some type of relationship between salesperson and prospect. When you develop a strong relationship there is a greater chance that your prospect will choose your product or service over your competitors.

So, how do you develop this relationship?

Like anything any relationship, the selling relationship is built on trust. That means that you need to cultivate that relationship by:

- Showing interest in your prospects' business.

- Demonstrating how you can help them achieve their goals and objectives.

- Keeping in touch with them on a regular basis without trying to sell them something.

- Connecting them with other people who can help them with their business.

It is not easy to develop close relationships with business executives or buyers. However, when you focus on their needs instead of yours, a strong relationship is more likely to develop. A good friend of mine is a master at developing these types of relationships. He constantly looks for ways to help his clients achieve their goals. He contemplates different strategies, thinks outside the box, and tries to figure out unique approaches. Plus, he is willing to go the extra mile, which demonstrates his desire to help his clients.

SALES TIP

What can you do to improve your relationships with your existing clients *and* potential customers?

THE POWER OF SAYING NO

"You must consciously and consistently abandon business."
Alan Weiss, *Million Dollar Consulting*

Sometimes it makes good business sense to say no. When I first began my private practice, I took on almost every job that came my way. In a few situations, I delivered the program that was requested but knew that it wasn't my best work.

In fact, I once arranged to conduct a training workshop with a company I had been courting for over a year. As we got closer to the day of the workshop, I began to feel uneasy about the deal because of conversations I had with the owner. His behavior toward his sales team was less than professional, and I began to have concerns that my training would not have as much impact on their business as possible. These concerns were validated after the workshop was completed. I now make a point of refusing work that does not fall into my specific areas of expertise. Interestingly enough, it seems that when I turn away business I end up getting more calls in the days following.

- You can refuse to do business with companies who demonstrate unethical behavior.

- You can fire customers when they become too demanding.

- You can say no when your current workload will prevent you from meeting a deadline.

- You can say no to unrealistic demands.

- You can turn down requests to discount your products and services.

Too many salespeople feel that they have to agree to their customers' demands or to sell to everyone who expresses interest. The interesting thing with saying no is that in many cases you will generate more business from other sources immediately afterward.

Here are some tactful ways of saying no;

- When a client asks you for something that you don't offer: "I'd really like to do that, however, that's not a service we provide."

- Instead of saying no to a deadline, you can say, "I'm not sure I can meet that deadline. Would it be okay if we pushed it back two days?"

- When asked for a discount, "That price isn't possible—here's what I can do."

SALES TIP

Identify sales commitments you have made in the past that would have been better to turn down or refuse. Make a pact with yourself to say no if and when these situations arise in the future. Remind yourself that if you do not feel comfortable with the agreement, you should probably turn it down.

THE POWER OF
SCRIPTS

"The difference between sounding prepared and unprofessional is practice."
Kelley Robertson

If you make cold calls or deliver any type of sales presentation, I recommend you use some form of script. Most people shudder at the thought of using a script, thinking of the telemarketing calls they receive at eight in the evening and the mechanical tone of the callers.

However, scripts are very valuable when used properly. I must admit that I did not always think this way. In the spring of 1995, I began marketing my first seminar. It was geared toward the hospitality industry and was called *How to Make Incredible Tips*. I had no experience at cold calling so I bought a book I thought would help me.

The first concept introduced was to create an opening script. So, I wrote out a script that introduced me, my company, and what we did. The second principle instructed me to verbally practice this script until I was completely familiar with it, including the emphasis to place on each word and the tone. I read through the script several times until I thought I was ready to call the first number on my prospecting list. I picked up the phone and dialed. Surprisingly, I reached my prospect. That's when it happened.

I choked. I read my script instead of reciting it.

I stumbled and stammered several times until my prospect gruffly demanded, "What do you want?" At that point I tossed away my script, believing that scripts did not work. When I reflect on that experience I realize that the only person to blame was me. I did not practise my script until I was completely comfortable and familiar with it.

The objective of a script is to make your discussion of a topic more effective. The difference between an average salesperson and a sales professional is that the latter will rehearse her lines and deliver them the way they are meant to be delivered. I compare this to an amateur actor versus a Hollywood star. An experienced actor will place the right emphasis on the correct word, use the appropriate tone, and deliver his lines in a manner that will have you believing he is actually that character.

A well-practised script will sound natural. It will be convincing. It will be believable. I use scripts in the form of stories or anecdotes in most of my training workshops and keynote presentations. When I create a new presentation, I develop new stories (scripts) and practise them until I can tell the story in a convincing manner without stumbling or stammering. At that point, my script is ready. A short script takes less time to perfect than a five- or ten-minute story, but I have learned that practice is critical in both situations.

This concept also applies to your sales presentations. Most people do not give a sales presentation much thought. They ask a few questions, then launch into a discussion about their product or service. However, they do not invest the time practising their presentation, and just wing it instead. They may cover most of the relevant information, but their presentation will not have the impact it could have had they created a script.

SALES TIP

What story, key point, or message do you want to deliver? Create a script for your key message and practise it until it sounds exactly the way you want it to.

THE POWER OF SELF-EVALUATION

"Criticism may not be agreeable, but it is necessary.
It fulfils the same function as pain in the human body.
It calls attention to an unhealthy state of things."
Winston Churchill

I don't think there is such a thing as a perfect sales call or presentation and I believe that we can always improve our performance. Conducting a self-evaluation after each sales call or presentation is one of the best ways to improve your performance. You have a couple of options available to you:

1. Record your conversations with prospects and customers. Invest in a small voice recorder and use it when you have face-to-face meetings. You can also record your telephone calls, which helps you hear exactly how you come across to other people.

2. Write a self-evaluation.

Here are three questions you can ask that will help you evaluate your performance:

1. What did I do well? This question accentuates the positive aspect of your sales approach. I believe we should focus on the things we do well, and we should continue to do them.

2. What did I miss or forget to do? No sales call or interaction is perfect, which means it is important to assess the areas we can

improve. Many years ago I used to record the answers to this question after every training workshop. After a period of time I reviewed my responses and noticed several inconsistencies. I modified my approach and achieved better results.

3. What would I do differently in the future? This questions helps focus attention on the future and what changes in behavior will make a positive impact.

Very few people actually take the time to critique their performance during a sales call or meeting. However, critiquing your performance can help you make significant improvements in your results.

SALES TIP

Invest a few minutes to critique your performance immediately after every sales call, interaction, meeting, or presentation. Record your comments in a journal or binder and review them regularly. Watch for inconsistencies and take action to correct shortcomings.

THE POWER OF SEMINARS

"Seminars are one of the best ways to position yourself as an expert."

Seminars are an excellent way to demonstrate your knowledge and how you can help your prospective customers. Sales professionals in many industries conduct seminars, invite people to attend, and create new customers. I have invited prospective clients to my public seminars so they can experience first-hand my expertise and how I typically run a workshop. I usually generate at least one new client from these public seminars.

A close friend of mine is a financial planner, and he used to conduct free seminars on a regular basis. He would offer valuable information to the people who attended and he consistently developed new clients and generated additional business immediately after the seminar.

Many retailers use this approach. Home Depot offers weekly seminars on home improvement techniques. Paint stores show people how to create different looks and finishes. Electronics stores demonstrate how to maximize the use of your digital equipment or how to buy a home theater system. I once spoke to one of my competitors who conducted several showcase presentations each year. I was amazed to learn that he usually ended up doing business with more than fifty percent of the people in attendance at these free programs.

This is not an inexpensive way to generate new sales. However, it can be extremely effective because people see you in action. They can see your value. The costs associated with this approach include:

- A meeting space. This is often a hotel meeting room, which means paying anywhere from $100 to $500, depending on the size of group you anticipate, the length of the seminar, and the location. If you work for a large company, you may be able to use a meeting room in their office, which automatically reduces your costs.

- Refreshments. You will want to provide coffee, tea, soda, water, and perhaps some type of snack depending on the time of day you schedule your seminar.

- An advertising campaign. This is usually the biggest expense. The typical response rate for a direct-mail campaign is less than three percent, which means you need to send out a lot of letters to generate a sufficient level of attendance. However, if you have a good mailing list, you will likely generate a higher response.

A way to reduce your costs is to deliver your seminar at an industry conference. Most associations and industries hold regular conferences and are constantly seeking people to deliver programs and seminars. The association covers the cost of the meeting room, the marketing of the event, and often the printing of materials. That means your only expense is the travel to and from the event and the time to deliver your presentation.

It is also critical to plan your seminar well ahead of time. Give yourself at least two months of lead time. This will give you time to inform people, prepare your presentation, and make the necessary arrangements. You must have a well-developed presentation, quality handouts, and something of value to offer people.

Your presentation cannot be a blatant advertisement for your company and/or business. You can mention what you do, who your clients are, and how they have benefited. But you cannot stand in front of the group and make this seminar a one- to six-hour advertisement.

Although a seminar is more challenging to implement than other strategies in this book, it is very effective at generating new clients and business.

SALES TIP

If you have a product or service that lends itself to this concept, decide what type of seminar you can create. When you market it, make sure you focus on the benefits to the attendees. Keep the cost reasonable, if not free, to ensure great attendance.

THE POWER OF SHOWING VALUE

"Value is what you get."
Warren Buffett

You have no doubt heard the expression "value-added selling." I think this phrase is overworked and overused in today's business environment. However, I also know from personal experience that people want value for their money. Whether you sell directly to consumers or business to business, all your clients want value in their purchases.

The key is to determine exactly what value means to each and every customer. It may mean 24/7 support. It could be the reliability of your product. It might be the ease of installation or integration of your product into the customer's existing system. It could be that you offer flexible payment terms or provide excellent technical support.

That's why you need to ask questions—early in the sales process. Asking the right questions helps you determine what is important to each customer. You can then demonstrate the value of buying your particular product or service.

In some of my workshops I have participants create a list of services they provide to their customers. I ask them to attach a dollar figure to each item. This acts as a reminder of the value they offer. You can do the same with your business. Identify the things you do that have value for your customers, and attach a dollar figure to them. When faced with resistance, you can refer to this list and help your customer see why it makes sense to do business with you. One caution with this approach—avoid stating every item in order to capture the sale. Instead, highlight key points that are relevant to each particular customer. This will have more impact than reciting every point.

Although price is a factor in every sale, it is seldom the primary or motivating factor. However, in order to demonstrate your value you must avoid discussing price too early in the sales process—a mistake that most salespeople are guilty of making. Here is an example from my business.

A typical request for speaking or training starts with an e-mail or voice-mail message like, "Hi, we're interested in bringing in a speaker to discuss sales/negotiating/coaching/customer service skills. How much do you charge?"

Instead of stating my price immediately, I ask for more information. If I'm responding to an e-mail, I will request a telephone meeting with my prospect. During the telephone conversation I will find out what the prospect hopes to achieve, who else is involved in the decision, how many people will attend the session, where it will be held, the goals of the company as they relate to the session, as well as a few other details that help me determine what approach to take. If I can't arrange a telephone conversation, I will ask for additional information before I offer a solution or state my fees.

I have consistently found that the more time I invest learning about my prospect's needs, the better job I can do showing the value that I bring to the equation.

SALES TIP

Identify the value you bring to your client's situation. Then, determine the best way to present the value of your product or service to your customers and prospects.

THE POWER OF
SILENCE

"Silence is a source of great strength."
Lao Tzu

Silence is a one of the most powerful sales tools you can use because it makes most people feel uncomfortable. Unfortunately, most salespeople talk too much. They think that telling is selling when, in fact, allowing the customer to talk will gain them more sales. I personally believe that a sales professional should do less than thirty percent of the talking, which means salespeople need to develop the habit and skill of remaining silent.

When I worked in the hospitality industry I had a boss who would often use a pregnant pause when interviewing potential candidates. After candidates responded to a question, my manager would smile, nod, and wait expectantly. In all but a few cases, people blurted out additional information my manager would not have learned otherwise. People are uncomfortable with silence, which means they will usually fill up dead-air space by talking. And the more they talk, the sooner you may reach an agreement and close the sale.

Teach yourself to pause for a few seconds before you respond to a customer's request. You will often find that she will make a concession or give you more information that will help you in the sales process. I remember watching my wife in a retail store. She made a comment about the price and remained completely silent as the salesperson talked. She shook her head a few times and within a few minutes, the salesperson offered her a much better price.

It is critical that you remain silent after you ask any type of question, including asking for the sale. People need time to process information and come up with a response. In some cases, it may take twenty to thirty seconds for people to compose a response to your question, which means that if you speak during this time you interrupt their train of thought.

SALES TIP

Practise asking for the sale and remaining silent until your customer responds. This one step is guaranteed to increase your sales.

THE POWER OF
SMALL TALK

"Knowing when to engage a customer or
prospect in small talk is a master sales skill."
Kelley Robertson

Can you make small talk with someone? Do you find it easy or difficult to engage in social chatter with a stranger? Can you speak intelligently on a variety of topics?

If you want to improve your sales, focus on improving your ability to carry on a conversation with someone you don't know. This social chatter or small talk can often make or break the sale.

I remember one of my first sales calls many years ago. I met with the owner of a new restaurant to discuss the possibility of training their staff. He started talking about the weather, sports, and a few current events. Before long, I directed the conversation to the primary reason for our meeting. I noticed that he seemed a bit put off by this approach, and he closed up somewhat. I found out later that he gauged a salesperson's effectiveness by his or her ability to make small talk. He needed to establish some form of relationship with people before he would make a buying decision, and my haste to cut to the chase almost cost me the sale.

Be prepared to speak on a range of issues by reading the daily newspaper or watching the morning news. An awareness of current affairs will enable you to engage in a conversation with virtually anyone. I once had a boss who knew something about almost everything. He was extremely well versed and well read and could carry on a conversation on almost any topic. This approach helped him connect with people at every level within the company and certainly contributed to his success.

SALES TIP

Invest time expanding your horizons and knowledge of different subjects. You don't need to become an expert on everything but if you can talk about a wide range of topics, you will gain your customers' respect.

THE POWER OF STORIES

"Storytelling is the most powerful way to put ideas into the world today."
Robert McAfee Brown

Hundreds of years ago, storytellers would travel from city to city. They would weave tales and stimulate their listeners by capturing their imaginations. As a professional speaker I have learned that people remember stories more than anything else. In fact, I often have people come up to me and ask if I still tell a specific story in one of my workshops.

I remember attending a sales-training program a few years ago and the presenter discussed the impact a story can have in a sales presentation. The story can be an example of how someone achieved better results by using your product or service. You can use names, figures, statistics, and so on. However, do not make up or create a fictional situation. In most cases, your prospects will pick up on this and you will lose credibility.

My wife and I were once shopping for some new furniture, and she asked the salesperson a question about the fabric. He responded by telling us a story of another customer who had spilled wine on the fabric and how easily the fabric cleaned up. This helped us visualize the experience and made it easy for us to connect with his comments.

SALES TIP

Develop a series of stories you can use to reinforce key points of your sales presentation.

THE POWER OF STRUCTURE

*"Innovation is not the product of logical thought,
although the result is tied to logical structure."*
Albert Einstein

Structure is very important in the sales process. Without some form of structure you are more likely going to wing it during a conversation with a prospect or customer. Even if you have been successful using this approach, I will suggest that you are achieving the sales you are capable of. I'm not suggesting that every step in the sales process be scripted. But knowing where you are in the process will help you determine what to do next.

In my first book, *Stop, Ask and Listen—Proven Sales Techniques to Turn Browsers into Buyers*, I introduced the GUEST model of selling. This acronym means:

Greeting your customers

Uncovering their needs

Explaining your product or service

Solving objections

Telling them to buy

Although this process was originally written with retailers in mind, it applies to virtually anyone who sells a product or service. Following a structured process gives you a beginning, middle, and an end. Here are the three key parts of a structured sales interaction.

It begins with the initial contact with the prospect or customer. Your goal is to begin creating a connection with the prospect so the prospect feels comfortable with you. As stated in Secret #35—The Power of First Impressions, you have exactly one opportunity to make a great first impression, and that impression will influence the customer's decision to do business with you.

In the middle part of the process you ask questions and learn as much as you can about your customer's situation, needs, and wants. This is, without a doubt, the most important aspect of any sales conversation. Asking high-quality, thought-provoking questions will help you gather the necessary information so you can effectively position your products or services.

Also in the middle part of the process you present your solution—you demonstrate how your product or service will solve the current problems your prospect is experiencing. Presentation of your solution may consist of a short discussion, a more formal presentation to a committee, or a written proposal.

The final component is gaining some form of commitment. Regardless of what you sell and to whom, it is essential that you end every sales conversation with this step. With a simple purchase, it can be a matter of asking that person to make a buying decision. In a more complex or complicated sales process, it may be arranging the next steps or scheduling a meeting with other people involved in the purchase.

SALES TIP

Begin incorporating some form of structure into your sales interactions. Write down the steps you typically follow with new prospects and create a process that you can use and follow. Incorporating structure into a sales process will help keep you on track.

THE POWER OF SUGGESTION

"I'd asked around 10 or 15 people for suggestions.
Finally one lady friend asked the right question,
'Well, what do you love most?'
That's how I started painting money."
Andy Warhol

In many situations, people want your suggestions. Many salespeople feel uncomfortable suggesting specific solutions because they are hesitant about making the decision for their customer. However, if someone asks you, it means you have earned that customer's trust. And, if you have asked the right questions and listened to the answers, you should be able to recommend a solution.

When I first started my private practice, I always gave my customer several choices and frequently found that they asked which one I would recommend, sometimes prefacing their question with, "You're the expert, what do you think?" Over the years I have become more comfortable making specific suggestions and have found that I can be quite direct when mentioning them.

If you have regular customers and have sold them a variety of products or services in the past, it is usually easier to use this approach. You have likely developed a good relationship with them, learned more about their business, and better understand their situation now than when you first starting doing business with them. Assuming your products and services have met their expectations, you are in a position to make suggestions, and your customers will be more prone to accepting them.

SALES TIP

Be prepared to make specific suggestions when your customer asks. If you have asked the appropriate questions and know enough about the customer's situation, you should be able to make a recommendation.

THE POWER OF SUMMARIZING

"Eighty percent of buyers felt that summarizing a meeting's key points was extremely important. However, only 54% of sales reps take the time to summarize."
Michael Schell, *Buyer Approved Selling*

Summarizing is a tool that is underutilized by many sales professionals. This technique can be used at several different times during the sales interaction.

The first opportunity is after you have invested time learning about your customer's situation. Once you've asked the right questions, listened to your customer's response, and fully understood what he needs and wants, you should verbally summarize the information.

- "From what you've told me here's what you are looking for in a washer. You want an extra large basin, an alarm to indicate the end of the cycle, and... Is that right?"

- "So based on what you've said, these are the most important aspects of this purchase. You want... Would that be accurate?"

Summarizing at the end of the qualifying process is an important step. It shows that you've listened to your customer. It helps him confirm what he is looking for. If you have accidentally missed anything important the customer will generally speak up and say, "Oh, I also want..." Summarizing also helps you determine if you've thoroughly understood the customer and his specific situation.

You should summarize when you have concluded your presentation. Let's say you have spent twenty or thirty minutes showing your prospect how your particular product will benefit her. At this time, it is important to recap what you have told her. This can be done in point form, and should include each of the benefits your product offers. You can say, "Ms. Prospect, I have covered quite a bit of information so far. Let me take a moment to recap what I've said. This particular unit will allow you to..." This approach definitely makes it easier for your customer to remember everything you have told her.

A third opportunity to summarize is when you forget the next part of your presentation. It is not uncommon for anyone to forget aspects of the sales presentation. Instead of forcing yourself to try to remember what to say next, simply restate what you have discussed thus far. This will help your brain get back on track and will allow you to continue your presentation.

Last, summarizing is also helpful just before you ask for the sale. You can summarize the key points of your presentation then ask your customer or prospect for a buying decision.

SALES TIP

Practise summarizing during these four points of your sales calls and meetings. Start with summarizing your understanding of the customer's needs and current situation. Next, focus on recapping your presentation. If you happen to forget part of your sales presentation, take a moment and summarize what you just said. Last, summarize just before you ask for the sale.

THE POWER OF
TELEPHONE SKILLS

"If e-mail had been around before the telephone was invented people would have said, 'Hey, forget e-mail—with this new telephone invention I can actually talk to people."

Everyone who sells for a living must use the telephone from time to time. You may not cold call but you will have to talk to clients. And great telephone skills reflect your professionalism.

Unlike face-to-face meetings, telephone conversations do not provide the opportunity to see the person. According to studies, our tone of voice accounts for eighty-three percent of our message when we talk on the telephone, and our words account for seventeen percent, compared to thirty-eight percent and seven percent respectively when speaking face to face. That means we need to be even more aware of our tone of voice and the words we choose. Here are a few of the mistakes I hear salespeople make during telephone conversations:

- Not using the appropriate pace. If you have a tendency to speak quickly, make the effort to slow down, particularly when you are leaving a message and expect a return call. Most people who call me and leave voice-mail messages recite their telephone numbers too quickly for me to write them down. I have to listen to their message again to capture their number. I have also experienced situations when the caller states the company name so quickly it is impossible to decipher. Remember, your goal is to make it easy for people to do business with you.

- Failing to pause before responding to the other person's comments or questions. The pause ensures that the other person has completed her thought and prevents you from unintentionally interrupting her.

- Working on the computer during the conversation. I recall speaking to a salesperson and hearing him typing furiously away on his computer. This was not only distracting to me; I also felt it showed signs of disrespect. However, if he had said, "I'm just going to record your information while we speak," it might have changed my perception.

Call center experts suggest that you place a mirror on your desk so you can see your facial expressions when speaking on the telephone.

SALES TIP

Record your next telephone sales call and listen to it afterward. Pay attention to how relaxed or stressed you sound and whether or not you sound like you are trying to sell something.

THE POWER OF "TELL ME"

"People will tell you anything you want to know. All you have to do is ask."
Kelley Robertson

"Tell me" is an excellent way to encourage people to share information with you. The "tell-me" approach is extremely effective because it allows you to gather the information you need to help your customer make an educated buying decision, but it is less intrusive than asking a series of questions. Most people will openly respond to this approach because they do not feel as if they are being questioned—sometimes people will get defensive if they feel they are being interrogated. Here are a few examples:

"Tell me about your current situation."
"Tell me what is important to you in this purchase."
"Tell me what features you want in this system."
"Tell me about your event."
"Tell me who else you typically speak to when you make a decision like this."
"Tell me what concerns you have."
"Tell me what you would like to see upgraded."
"Tell me what changes you would like to have in a new system."
"Tell me how your company usually makes decisions of this nature."
"Tell me what other companies you are speaking to about this."
"Tell me how you want this system installed."

"Tell me when you were planning to make this decision."

"Tell me what prompted you to call me/us."

SALES TIP

Develop a list of "tell-me" questions you can use in your business and start using them in your next conversation with a prospective customer.

THE POWER OF TESTIMONIALS

"People believe what they read more than what they hear."

Testimonials have a tremendous ability to influence buying decisions, and great salespeople and marketers know how important testimonials and endorsements are to their business. If you watch television you will notice that every infomercial includes several testimonials, often from celebrities.

I'm not suggesting that you need celebrity endorsements to successfully sell your product or service. However, the endorsement is frequently underutilized because we don't know how to ask for a testimonial or endorsement. We do not want to sound needy or pushy; nor do we want to cause any inconvenience for our customers.

Here are a few suggestions that can help.

1. When you have reached an agreement with your client but before you have delivered your product or service, you can tell the client that you will be asking for a testimonial once the sale has been completed. You can say something like this: "Mr. Client, my goal is to make sure you are completely satisfied with the product/service I deliver. After you have implemented it, I'm going to ask you for a testimonial because I am confident you will be extremely satisfied with it." You have now established an expectation in his mind, and you will likely

make sure that you deliver as promised (or more). When you complete the work, contact your client and say, "I trust you are satisfied with our work and that we have delivered on our promises. Would you be willing to jot down a few words on letterhead for me?"

2. Another technique is to listen to the comments your clients make during conversations. When they make favorable comments you can ask if they would be willing to write them down for you. I have used this approach after conducting workshops for my clients. In one particular situation, my client said he was amazed at the improvement of his team's presentation skills after completing my workshop. He willingly agreed to record his comments on letterhead, and I now use that letter when I talk to prospective clients about this workshop.

3. You can also ask a third party to contact your customers and ask for a verbal testimonial. Record these in digital format and, after you have collected several, you can place them on an audio CD. You can also put these comments on your web site so visitors can hear what your clients think.

Sometimes your clients won't know exactly what to say, so you can give them some prompting. Ask them to focus on topics such as cost reductions, increases in sales, on-time (and on-budget) completion of projects, your flexibility in developing a solution, and so on.

You can, and should, use testimonials on your web site, in your brochures, when you submit proposals, in e-mail signature files, and when you meet a new prospect for the first time. You can use written letters, audio recordings, and even videotaped endorsements.

Take the time to watch a few dozen infomercials. Surf the Internet and read the endorsements on web sites. Read the back covers of books to see what readers of that book have had to say. Use each of these to determine what type of testimonial would work best for your business. Rather than telling people how good your product or service is, have others do it for you.

SALES TIP

Decide what you want people to say about your products or services. Create a list of customers who would be willing to give you an endorsement. Next, determine what media work best for you (written, audio, video). Then start taking action to get these testimonials.

THE POWER OF
THANK-YOU CARDS

"When did you last receive a thank-you card from someone other than your Mom?"
Kelley Robertson

Thank-you cards can be powerful sales tools because they can help you differentiate yourself from your competitors. There are several opportunities to send people a thank-you card.

- After an initial face-to-face meeting or sales call. When you leave a prospect's office and return to work, take a few moments to write a brief thank-you card. Tell your prospects that you enjoyed meeting her and learning more about her specific goals, objectives, or business. Then mention that you look forward to working with her in the future.

- When you receive payment for an invoice. Demonstrate your appreciation for on-time payment of an invoice by sending a thank-you card.

- After a client has agreed to do business with you (signing a contract, verbal agreement, and so on). This will reinforce their decision and reduce buyer's remorse—both from a business-to-consumer and from a business-to-business environment.

- After a client has purchased and/or used your product or service. I think it is essential to demonstrate your appreciation of someone's purchase by sending her a thank-you card after she has made her purchase.

- When someone sends you a referral. I think it is critical to send a thank-you card to someone who referred another customer or client to you.

- When clients write or give you a testimonial or endorsement. If customers take the time and make the effort to write an endorsement for you, take the time to thank them. This will confirm that their decision to help you was a wise one.

- When they decline to use your product or service. When someone decides against using your product or service, sending a thank-you card demonstrates a high level of professionalism. Very few, if any, salespeople send cards *after* they have been rejected, so such a card can help you stand out from the crowd.

Thank-you cards should be handwritten, and I strongly recommend using letter mail versus e-mail. Most people are inundated with e-mail, and a handwritten card will stand out when it is received and read by your customer or prospect. In fact, most people end up keeping these cards, because they seldom receive cards of this nature except from relatives thanking them for a gift.

SALES TIP

Make a commitment to send out at least three to five thank-you cards every week. Look for reasons to send these cards and take initiative to make it happen.

THE POWER OF TIME MANAGEMENT

"Time is free, but it's priceless. You can't own it, but you can use it. You can't keep it, but you can spend it. Once you've lost it you can never get it back."
Harvey MacKay, *Swim with the Sharks*

Effective selling requires effective time-management skills. You need to know how to maximize the use of your time and prioritize your selling day. Many salespeople engage in too many non-selling-related activities during peak selling time. Activities such as paperwork and administrative duties can easily occupy your day, which limits your ability to maximize your sales. Here are three key tips that will help you make the most of your day.

1. **Use a to-do list every day.** This one step will help you improve your productivity immediately. On a sheet of paper or in your electronic organizer, list all the tasks you need to complete. For best results, create a few categories, such as e-mail, calls, and projects. Using the list prevents you from forgetting tasks and helps keep you on track. Cross off each item as you complete it and move to the next item on your list.

2. **Prioritize your tasks.** One of the biggest mistakes people make is to work on the easiest tasks first. This is called the path of least resistance. However, in most cases, the easy items are not as important to your overall success as other tasks. But we tend to tackle them first because they are easier to do or because we

enjoy doing them. Then, at the end of the day, we find the most important items still on our list and we wonder where the day went.

The most effective way to prioritize your list is to label each item with an A, B, or C. A items are critical—must be done. B tasks are important, and C items are the least important. Once you have labelled each item on your list, prioritize them using numbers. Review your A list and determine which task is the most important, the second most important, and so on. This process takes less than one or two minutes but will usually improve your productivity by as much as thirty percent.

3. **Set aside a specific time to read, listen to, and respond to e-mail and voice mail.** This is particularly effective when you are working on a project that requires a lot of focus. I usually turn off my telephone and close my e-mail program when I am working on a project that takes considerable mental effort. Rather than have my concentration broken by technology, I can focus on finishing the task undisturbed. It is tempting to stay connected at all times, but I have learned that being connected is a distraction.

Time expands or contracts in relation to the deadlines we set for ourselves. When we need to accomplish a task by a specific time we tend to focus more intently on finishing that particular piece of work.

SALES TIP

Incorporate these simple techniques into your daily routine and you will experience an immediate improvement in your productivity.

THE POWER OF TRUST

"The most important thing we sell is trust."
Tom Stoyan, *Canada's Sales Coach*

If a prospect does not trust you, you will not close the sale. Selling is an honorable profession, providing you behave in an honest and ethical manner. Misleading someone, even slightly, is not professional.

It amazes me how many salespeople have no hesitation about stretching the truth so they can close the sale. While this may work to get the initial sale, it is seldom an effective long-term approach.

Everything you do will either increase or reduce the level of trust you develop with your customers and prospects. Examples include:

- the speed with which you respond to requests
- how you treat clients' employees, including receptionists and mailroom staff
- the manner in which you answer e-mails and telephone calls
- your attention to details
- how clearly you convey your message
- eye contact
- doing what you say you will do when you say you will do it
- underpromising and overdelivering

- not making outlandish claims about your product or service

- listening carefully to your customer

- not attempting to sell your prospect something he or she doesn't need or want

- not pushing unwanted services

SALES TIP

What can you do to create a high level of trust with your customers and prospects?

THE POWER OF UP-SELLING

"Would you like fries with that?"
McDonald's employee

In today's competitive business environment, sales and profitability are ongoing concerns for most companies. Shareholder and/or corporate expectations of a healthy return on investment and consumer demands for lower prices appear to be diametrically opposed. There is, however, a way to survive the pressure from these demands.

Sell more add-ons, accessories, or additional services.

This may appear to be a simplistic approach, but the truth is that most salespeople miss many sales opportunities because they neglect to actively sell additional high-margin items. These items contribute immediately to top-end sales and bottom-line profitability.

I have heard excuses such as:

- "I don't have time."

- "Customers will tell me if they want anything else."

- "I'm concerned customers will think I'm being pushy."

- "I'm afraid of losing the sale." (Particularly for commissioned salespeople)

- "I don't get paid commissions so why bother?"

I'll reference McDonald's, the burger giant, to address some of these and other excuses:

"I don't have time."

When the counter person asks, "Would you like fries with that?" it takes exactly 1.4 seconds. Suggesting add-ons does *not* take much extra time, particularly when you consider the potential payoff.

"I don't get paid commissions..."

You or your employee(s) may not make commissions. Neither do the counter clerks at McDonald's, and yet they still suggest a large order of fries or a dessert.

"My store is too busy."

See response to "I don't have time."

Now, let me deal with the remaining objections by relating some personal experiences.

"Customers will tell me if they want anything else."

When my wife and I bought our first computer we could hardly wait to get home and set it up. However, when I went to plug in the last power cord I was lacking a receptacle. I needed a power bar. This didn't even cross my mind when I was in the computer store, but if the salesperson had suggested it, I would have bought one.

"I'm concerned customers will think I'm being pushy."

Several years ago I was shopping for new suits. The sales staff brought me shirts, ties, and socks to complement my suits. When I left the store I was excited because I knew I had several combinations of suits, shirts, and ties to wear. Not once did I feel that the salespeople were pushing me into buying something I didn't want or need.

"I'm afraid of losing the sale."

In the example above, I didn't even consider *not* buying the suits because the salespeople were assertively accessorizing. I wanted and needed the suits and I had already invested a significant amount of time in the buying process.

SALES TIP

Do yourself a favor and start suggesting additional products and services to your customers. Execute consistently, and watch your sales and profitability increase.

THE POWER OF VISIBILITY

"It isn't just what you know, and it isn't just who you know. It's actually who you know, who knows you, and what you do for a living."
Bob Burg

You may have the best product or the most unique service on the market. But, if no one knows who you are, you may not succeed.

How do you make yourself visible? You have a variety of options available that do not cost a lot of money.

Advertising. This is often perceived as the most expensive way to create awareness. However, you can advertise in magazines at little or no charge. One way is to write an article in exchange for an ad. I have successfully done this many times. My article is featured in a magazine plus I get to place an ad in that publication at no charge. As I mentioned earlier in this book, most trade publications are hungry for good content but they don't have the budget to pay professional freelance writers. In many cases, they are willing to exchange a small ad for a quality article.

Affiliate programs. In an affiliate program, you refer business to a particular company in exchange for a commission. I have asked people to advertise or promote my public workshops, and in return they receive a commission for anyone who registers for my workshop. What noncompeting businesses can you link with that will help you increase your visibility?

Articles. Trade magazines, local newspapers, electronic newsletters, and web sites all want content that will help their readers and subscribers. Write a short article that offers practical advice and submit it to a variety of publications. As long as it is not a blatant advertisement for your company, there is a good chance it will be printed. Include a brief bio and contact information.

Blogs. A blog, or web log, can be a great way to create visibility for your company, products, and services. Essentially, a blog gives you the opportunity to provide information about and promote your products at the same time. The great thing about blogs is that they are easy to create and maintain. You can have a blog up and running in a matter of a few minutes, and at no cost. You can visit my blogs at http://kelleyrobertson. blogspot.com. Here you will find postings about sales, negotiating, and customer service. Or visit http://secretsofpowerselling.blogspot.com for updates on this book.

Chat rooms. Chat rooms on virtually every topic abound on the Internet. Surf the Net and look for the opportunities. You cannot pitch your product but, as with articles, you can offer feedback, help people with their challenges, and give them direction.

Existing clientele. Make sure you tell your customers and clients of the other products you offer. More often than not, your clients are not aware of the other services you offer. I experienced this recently when I was talking to a new prospect. I made a comment about a program I delivered for another customer, and my new prospect immediately showed interest. You can also ask clients to feature you in their corporate newsletter or web site, to increase your visibility and exposure.

Internet forums. Like chat rooms, the forums give you the opportunity to provide feedback and advice. In some cases, other forum members may contact you for additional products and services.

Interviews. You can work with a publicist and conduct radio, television, or Internet interviews. The interviews can expose you to a wide range of people and can generate leads. Make sure your interview focuses on helping your intended market with a particular problem.

Networking. When you attend a networking event, make sure you have a thirty- to sixty-second commercial ready. Tell people what you do and how you help your clients achieve results.

Newsletters. I mentioned this strategy earlier in the book. It has been one of the most effective ways for me to increase my visibility.

Referrals. This works two ways. Most people spend most of their time asking and looking for referrals. I have found that it is more effective to give someone else a referral. That person is then more likely to look for opportunities to give you a referral, which can mean more money in your pocket. I also think it is important to show your gratitude for a referral by giving the referrer some type of commission or referral fee. This shows that you are grateful for the additional business and will likely encourage additional referrals.

Search engines. If you are self-employed and have a web site, you should consider developing a strategy that utilizes search engines. With a well-crafted web site or an investment of a few hundred dollars a month you can drive more traffic to your site. One word of advice: this is a long-term strategy, so do not expect an immediate pay-off. Plus, your web site *must* be extremely well created and designed in order to generate business.

Speaking. This is one of the best ways to create visibility. Rotary and Lion's clubs are always looking for speakers at their meetings. Presentations for these organizations are usually between twenty and thirty minutes. Associations also want speakers who can offer practical advice to their members. You can expect a presentation about practical advice to last approximately sixty minutes. See Secret #68—The Power of Presentations for information on developing your presentation.

THE POWER OF VISION

"We are limited, not by our abilities, but by our vision."

Do you know where you're going? Do you know what you stand for? If not, take some time to figure this out, because it can help you in making decisions about your business.

I once had the good fortune to work for an outstanding leader who had the insight to develop a clear vision for our company. Within this vision he had four key strategic steps. Every decision that was made in our company was checked to see if it was consistent with the vision. If the solution helped us achieve our mission, we moved forward. If the project or solution did not help us move toward our goals, we declined. This simple process helped us make the right business decisions time and again.

As a sales professional, you should develop a clear vision of what you want to accomplish, who your client is, how you will conduct your business, and how you will treat your customers.

A vision should not be a lengthy paragraph with wishy-washy, feel-good propaganda. Your vision should clearly define you, your business, and what you hope to accomplish. In fact, the shorter the better. A brief eight- to fifteen-word statement can clearly identify you and your business. And it can help you keep focused.

Here are a few examples to help get you started.

"To be the premiere retail training company in North America."

"To be the most reputable furniture design company in the province."

"To provide the best-quality widgets in the industry."

"To be recognized as the leading supplier of widgets in the state."

What is your vision? What do you want to accomplish?

SALES TIP

Take time to figure out your vision. Don't try to figure out how you will achieve that vision—you will determine that later.

THE POWER OF VOICE MAIL

"Hi, this is Dale. I'm using voice mail to screen my calls to determine which ones have value to me."
Art Sobczak, *How to Sell More in Less Time with No Rejection*

There is no question that voice mail can be challenging to deal with. In my weekly newsletter I wrote a column about how to utilize voice mail more effectively and received this question from a subscriber:

We are the producers of two annual publications designed to meet the needs of a specific target market. For this reason, we are very selective in who we approach to participate in our publication. We research potential clients to ensure our publications speak to their target audience. However, it seems that businesses are so inundated with advertising sales opportunities and hounded by nuisance callers that they place all advertising salespersons in one basket and have labeled the basket "ignore at all cost." They ignore your phone messages and if you do manage to reach them, they have a very rude and negative attitude as a result of your persistence. I know a good salesperson should be able to work through this, but I have to tell you by the end of the day I begin to feel very unworthy. It is very hard to keep a positive attitude and a smile in your voice when you are treated so badly. I know I have a good product. But trying to get that message across to our potential clients is very difficult when they automatically put you in the same basket as the "nuisance" callers.

Feeling Unworthy

Here is the response I offered.

Dear Unworthy;

I know exactly how you feel. I've also experienced feelings of unworthiness and frustration, particularly after making several dozen calls in a day and making absolutely no progress!

Salespeople often forget that decision-makers in the corporate world are extremely busy. They are expected to do more with less, they are involved in projects and initiatives that occupy a substantial amount of time, and they attend more meetings than ever before. In fact, I recently spoke to an individual who said, "Just when I thought I couldn't possibly get any busier, I did." Finally, they are inundated with calls from people, like ourselves, who want to sell them something. Keeping that in mind, you need to position yourself in a manner that gives them a reason to be interested in your offering.

First of all, you must use telephone scripts for every call. But unlike telemarketers who call you at home, you must rehearse these scripts so they sound natural and not like a sales call. Skip the idle chitchat and get to the point. Your opener should give them an idea of the results you've helped your clients achieve—increased sales, reduced expenses, improved productivity, and so on. Return on Investment (ROI) is the bottom line in business. Develop a series of voice-mail scripts. An associate of mine has fifteen different scripts, which allow him to leave a different message each time he contacts a prospective client. People are busy and don't have time to listen to a long, drawn-out message so keep it short—thirty seconds or less.

Recognize that there is no guaranteed way to ensure that people will call you back. Unless they happen to recognize a need for exactly what you are selling at the exact time you call, they will probably not return your call. A business executive once told me she wouldn't even entertain the idea of speaking to a new salesperson because she already had too much on her plate.

With respect to the rudeness factor, whether we like it or not, businesspeople do lump all people who market by telephone into the same category. I have to admit that I'm guilty of it when someone contacts me, particularly when I am extremely busy.

SALES TIP

Develop a thick skin and do not take the rejection or rude comments personally.

THE POWER OF WALKING AWAY

"The single most powerful tool for winning a negotiation is the ability to get up and walk away from the table without a deal."

Maintaining the ability to walk away from a sale gives you an incredible sense of empowerment, because most salespeople are afraid to turn down business. This is particularly true for people who run services business, such as consulting, coaching, and speaking businesses. The hesitation to turn away business can cost you money.

In virtually every sales training and negotiating workshop I conduct, I encounter people who have accepted business from a particular customer or organization and immediately regretted it because they knew it was the wrong decision. Either the people they were dealing with were high-maintenance—meaning they required lots of attention—or the company's values did not match the salesperson's.

The owner of a specialty retail store once told me she would accept any deal in order to prevent a customer from going to her competitor. But this doesn't always make good business sense. If you lose money on the sale, it is definitely better to send the customer to the competition.

You don't have to sell to everybody! In fact, by reducing the amount of time you spend with high-maintenance, low-profit customers, you free up time to focus your attention on people who will contribute profit to your bottom line. You are in business to make money, to turn a profit.

Even if you are one of thousands of people employed in an organization, if you are in a sales role, your goal is to help that company stay in business by contributing to their bottom line. And selling goods and services at cost does not achieve this goal.

SALES TIP

In each sales situation, determine the point at which you will walk away. It is better to determine this early in the sales process.

THE POWER OF
A WINNER'S ATTITUDE

"Nothing can stop the man with the right mental attitude from achieving his goal; nothing on earth can help the man with the wrong mental attitude."
Thomas Jefferson

People often complain about how competitive their marketplace is. Among other things, they gripe about their competitors' lower prices, lack of service, lack of integrity, and lack of knowledge. In essence, they use their competition as a crutch that prevents them from reaching their own sales targets and goals. This is a victim mentality.

However, I know many people who consistently exceed their sales quotas even though they face the same competition as their co-workers. And these individuals usually have much higher targets than most people in the company. One key difference between these people and everyone else is that they don't whine, gripe, and complain about the competition. They work hard and they work smart. They maintain a winner's attitude.

Think of the message people receive from you when you have a winner's attitude and not a loser mentality. Winners are poised. They attract attention. They exude a confidence that compels you to do business with them. And people want to do business with winners, not losers or victims.

Ultimately, your beliefs influence your behavior, and your behavior affects your results. I will never dispute the fact that competition is fierce. In fact, virtually every industry faces more competition every day, week, month, and year. However, winners don't focus on their competition; they concentrate on achieving their goals, objectives, and targets.

SALES TIP

Decide what you can do to outpace, outdistance, and outsell your competition. What separates you from them? What do you offer that they don't? What makes you unique?

ABOUT THE
AUTHOR

Kelley Robertson, president of the Robertson Training Group, has been helping people improve their skills for almost two decades. He began by training employees, managers, and owner/operators in the hospitality industry, then became manager of retail training for Sony Canada. Since 1995 he has conducted hundreds of sales training workshops and helped thousands of professionals improve their sales results.

His client list includes Canadian Carpet Centre, Crabtree & Evelyn, Heffner Lexus Toyota, Hillebrand Estates Wine, Home Hardware, J. Michaels, Nutrition House, Part Source, Peller Estates Winery, Rogers Video, Sangster's Health Centres, Sony Canada, Staples/Business Depot, Creative Outdoor Advertising, Daryl King Real Estate Group, Delta Resorts, Epic Plant Company, Larter Advertising, National Network of Embroidery Professionals, Nord Gear Canada, Preferred Nutrition, and Personal Service Coffee.

Kelley Robertson's articles are published in a variety of online and print magazines and newsletters such as *Auto Trim & Restyling News, BedTimes, Boating Industry Canada, Canadian Business Franchise, Canadian Natural Health Retailer, Canadian Women's Business, Canadian Vending, Dartnell's Selling, Graphic Arts, Home Business Magazine, Luggage, Leather & Accessories, National Tanning Training Institute, Professional Door Dealer, Professional Jewelers, Sales & Marketing (New Zealand), Sales Promotion, Selling Radio, Sleep Saavy, Sleep Products, Small Office Home Office, Smart Tan, SOHO Small Business, Staff Digest,* and *Tire News.*

Kelley Robertson can be reached at:

kelley@robertsontraininggroup.com.

MORE RESOURCES TO HELP YOU
INCREASE YOUR SALES

Go to my website for more ideas, tips, articles, and resources that will help you increase your sales and make more money.

www.RobertsonTrainingGroup.com

Here is an idea of what you will find.

Free! "59 Second Sales Tip" Newsletter
This newsletter offers one piece of practical sales and motivation advice delivered via e-mail directly to your in-box. Sign up for your free subscription and receive a special report, "100 Ways to Increase Your Sales" absolutely free.

Stop, Ask & Listen—Proven Sales Techniques to Turn Browsers into Buyers
Originally written for retailers, this book has helped thousands of sales professionals in a variety of industries improve their sales results. It details key selling techniques that can be used by virtually anyone who sells a product or service. The concepts are easy to use and Kelley gives you his unique Blueprint for Success. This step-by-step process clearly

outlines how to incorporate the ideas and principles contained in this book into your daily and weekly routine.

Secrets to Overcoming Objections

If you hear objections like, "I'll think about it," "I can get this cheaper at your competitor," and "I need to check with…" then you need this program. Kelley shares nine key principles that will not only help you overcome objections; they will teach you how to prevent many objections from actually occurring. Available as an e-book (downloadable file) or as an audio CD.

72 Ways to Negotiate More Effectively

Are you constantly faced with buyers asking for outrageous discounts, concessions, and demands? Learn how to improve your negotiating skills by using a variety of tactics and strategies. This program will help you increase your sales and drive more money to your bottom line. Available as an e-book or audio CD.

Negotiate Like a Pro

A comprehensive audio program that gives you virtually all of the information you need to negotiate more effectively. Learn what techniques and strategies professional sales people use to negotiate better deals for themselves. This package includes 5 audio CDs and 1 CD-ROM that contains complete transcripts, action plans, negotiating templates, and self-critiques.

Sales is NOT a Four-Letter Word!

This CD contains a live version of Kelley's signature keynote presentation and offers insights that make the sale process easier to manage and more comfortable. Listen to this energetic, lively, and engaging presentation on your way to sales calls and appointments and boost your skills and motivation.

Setting Powerful Goals

This recorded tele-seminar will explain how you can easily increase your revenues by setting goals and developing action plans. This powerful and insightful session will show you exactly how to create, execute, and achieve goals that will keep you motivated, excited, and help you become more successful. Available as an audio CD.

Special pricing is available for bulk purchases.
Please contact us at 905-633-7750.